The Aquinas Lecture, 1982

THE GIFT: CREATION

Under the auspices of the
Wisconsin-Alpha Chapter of Phi Sigma Tau

By
KENNETH L. SCHMITZ

MARQUETTE UNIVERSITY PRESS
MILWAUKEE
1982

MARQUETTE
UNIVERSITY
PRESS

© 2011 Marquette University Press
Milwaukee, Wisconsin 53201-3141
All rights reserved.
www.marquette.edu/mupress/

Aquinas Lecture 46 © 1982
Under the auspices of the
Wisconsin-Alpha Chapter of Phi Sigma Tau
ISBN-13: 9780874621495
ISBN-10: 0874621496

Second printing 1996
Third printing 2007
Fourth printing 2011
Fifth printing 2014
Sixth printing 2017

Association of American
University Presses

MARQUETTE UNIVERSITY PRESS
MILWAUKEE

The Association of Jesuit University Presses

To Lil:

There (in *Acts* 17:16-33) we read of that
wonderful scene at the Areopagus in Athens
when St. Paul brought something new to the
Greek philosophers, namely, the absolute
beginning to be of a creature totally dependent
for its being on a Creator or, in other words,
the very "newness" of the world itself.

Paul M. Byrne*

CONTENTS

Prefatory

The Wisconsin-Alpha Chapter of Phi Sigma Tau, the National Honor Society for Philosophy at Marquette University, each year invites a scholar to deliver a lecture in honor of St. Thomas Aquinas.

The 1982 Aquinas Lecture *The Gift: Creation* was delivered in the Todd Wehr Chemistry Building on Sunday, February 21, 1982, by Kenneth L. Schmitz, Professor of Philosophy at Trinity College and the Graduate School in the University of Toronto, where he is also cross-appointed to the Graduate Centre for the Study of Religion.

After completing his undergraduate studies at St. Thomas More College in the University of Saskatchewan, Professor Schmitz earned a Licentiate at the Pontifical Institute of Medieval Studies (1952) and a Ph. D. from the University of Toronto (1953). He has taught at Loyola University of Los Angeles, Marquette University, Indiana University and the Catholic University of America. He has done post-doctoral study in Germany at Freiburg-im-Breisgau and at the Hegel-Archiv in Bochum-Ruhr.

His publications on metaphysics, philosophy of religion, philosophical anthropology and German philosophy have appeared in *The Review of Metaphysics, The Journal of Philosophy, Thought, Man and World, International Journal for Philosophy of Religion, Religious Studies,* and *Dialectics and Humanism.*

Professor Schmitz has served as the president of the Hegel Society of America (1974-76), of the American Catholic Philosophical Association (1977-78), and of the Metaphysical Society of America (1978-80). He has been the chairman of the English language edition of *Communio: An International Catholic Review* (1978-82), as well as editorial consultant for *The New Scholasticism* and *Prisma* (Brazil).

He has participated in Dialogues with Marxist Academies of Science since 1978, specifically with delegations from Polish, Bulgarian and Hungarian Academies. He has participated in international symposia in Brazil, Mexico, Argentina, and Kenya.

To Kenneth L. Schmitz's distinguished list of publications, Phi Sigma Tau is pleased to add: *The Gift: Creation.*

THE GIFT: CREATION

An ancient Christian creed begins: "We believe in the Father almighty, creator of heaven and earth. . . ." To the Biblical religions of Judaism, Christianity and Islam the creation of the world is not a simple statement of fact; it is above all an acknowledgement of the Lordship of God. So that the energy of faith is rooted not in admiration for a miraculous fact, but in wonder before the Creator Himself. In recent times scholars have collected hundreds of ancient myths of origin from other religions, living and dead, myths told among different peoples, in every part of the world, in a veritable Babel of tongues. And so we can speak of widespread memory of origins deeply rooted in the human heart and mind. And yet, what is there to remember? Were you there when the Lord laid down the foundations of the universe? More than one ancient myth begins: "Before there were animals and men. . . ." How, then, can we speak of memory? Is there, perhaps, within each of us a presence that draws us towards some great founding event? What is this "beginning" of which, in their different ways, the Bible and the ancient myths of origin speak, when they begin with the words: *In the beginning*. . . .

I

Among the living beings on our planet the human being is remarkable for his perception of time. Past and future open out to him as an indefinite expanse without beginning or end. And yet he somehow brings within his grasp the totality of time itself. Again and again, in a variety of ways, he has articulated myths of origin that take him back to the first time, and myths that take him forward to the last time. Or we might say that his temporal antennae reach backwards and forwards to a time beyond time, to a time of beginning and ending that is not simply continuous with the present time of days and nights, of weeks and months and years. In the myths of origin he enlarges the temporal horizon and touches the edge of a duration that precedes time itself. Scholars have helped us to recognize that cosmogonic myths are neither adventurous science nor unbridled fiction; and that they are meant to communicate the original and ultimate meaning of things and to provide human life with a guiding pattern. Archaic peoples showed a lively interest in the question of origins: of the coming to be of the world, the fashioning of man, the occurrence of evil, the coming of death, the emergence of important features of the environment, the generation of plants and animals, and the establishment of social institutions and customs. Some myths accept the existence of the world as given and go on to tell of the coming into being of man or of some special human quality (such as evil), some thing (such as a totem animal), some food (such as corn), or of some practice (such as ritual sacrifice). But many are properly cosmogonic and tell of the origin of the present world itself. Some say that at first nothing existed, neither stars, nor sun, nor moon; but they often add: there was only a watery abyss, or unrelieved darkness, thus expressing the notion of a primeval chaos. If they tell of a primordial sacred being, that shadowy presence is often alone; or there may be a first pair. Often the first creature to come into being is light. The means of creation are various: it may come about through mental activity, such as dreaming, imagining or willing; or through uttering a word. Or it may come about through sexual generation or some other bodily process; or yet again, through dismemberment or sacrifice; or through the activity of making, such as by molding clay.

To tell a myth of origin is to recount what has already occurred and has been told many times before. This "having been" is ingredient in the myth, for the recounting of the myth carries its hearers back to the remotest time, to a primordial past. Now such a past is no ordinary past. It is not the past that we recall as yesterday; nor is it the past described in history, nor the past reconstructed in archaeology, paleontology, geology or astro-physics. For these pasts are taken to be continuous with our present, and are cut from the same temporal thread. But the past of which the

myth speaks is *that* past, *illud tempus,* the first time,
the time of beginnings.[1] There is, then, discontinuity between the great shadowy figures and
events of the myth, the founding deeds, and these
present times. The time is so remote that it is utterly unlike these present times. Or, more precisely, it is not simply the remoteness of some "long
ago," but the "firstness" that lies at the threshold of
these present times. The time of beginning is
different in quality and kind, for it is original not
derived time, instituting not constituted time. It is
the time in which the great founding deeds were
done, — when earth split from sky, when a seed
began to grow in the watery waste, when the
monster was dismembered or the first ritual
sacrifice was performed, when the first parents
copulated, when the first dive was taken or the
cosmic egg first hatched.

This utter difference between the time of beginnings and the present time was distorted during
the quarrel between the pioneers of modern geology at the end of the eighteenth century and their
opponents, the Anti-uniformitarians. In support
of the geologists who preceded him Lyell argued[2]
that the new earth science must assume that the
movements that formed the mountains and val-
leys, rivers and oceans proceeded at the same rate
of motion as today's slow processes, so that they
must be measured according to the same measure
of time, even though this added many years to the
calculated age of the planet. The Anti-
uniformitarians or Catastrophists, on the other

hand, argued that creative time (the six "days" of *Genesis*) must be differentiated from the mundane time that followed (the four thousand years). The creative movement was catastrophic and to be measured by a different temporal rate. Now the Anti-uniformitarians noticed something distinctive about the time of beginnings, but they tried to incorporate creative and mundane time as two different rates within one continuum; and this confused both science and religion, as though they were part of the same explanatory enterprise. But today we understand better the significance of myths and that they do not require us to find a standard common to that time and these times. On the contrary, the myths declare their discontinuity with these present times. The cosmogonic myths speak out of a duration that precedes mundane time: "At that time even nothingness was not, nor existence. . . ," "Before the world was. . . ," "Before the beginning of the new-making. . . ," "Before there were animals or men. . . ," "In the beginning. . . ."[3] Such duration is heavy with the portents of creation, not measurable by ordinary time: infinite, eternal duration. There are myths that suppose an endless cycle of beginnings, of new worlds arising endlessly out of old worlds; but this chain simply compounds the difference by repeating it. It is because of this difference between primordial time and these present times that the myth can serve as a paradigm, a model to guide human action in these present times.[4] It is just the character *sui generis* of the original time that permits it to remain unabsorbed by the times that follow after it.

There is more to myths of origin, of course, than their discontinuity with present time, for the very telling of the myth is meant to provide an appropriate continuity as well, a sort of narrative bridge that is to take its hearers back to the primordial time, into the presence of those archetypal founding events in order to be renewed by their power. The retelling of the myth intends to communicate the freshness of that beginning, and to enable its hearers to participate in its creative energy. Performed in all its original seriousness the myth is a sacrament for the believing community. The "memory" invoked is a very special sort of "commemoration." The sacred story re-enacts the events through which the world has come to be and by which man has received existence and life, meaning and orientation. As with so many other religious activities, the telling of the myth is a coming together of opposites, *coincidentia oppositorum,* the coming together of discontinuity and continuity, of strangeness and familiarity. This coincidence is promoted by two features of the myth: its form and its power. The preterite character of primordial time, its absolute pastness, expresses itself in the narrative form of the myth; for the myth tells of events that have already happened. The preterite time and the narrative form give to the myth a certain completeness that makes it an apt vehicle for communicating the sacred fullness (completeness)

that invests it with paradigmatic power. The
sacred is true and unconditional existence; and it
is in virtue of this absolute fullness that a myth
can claim to be a paradigm for present and future
times. In sum, its temporal form, the perfect narrative past, is the *mode* of its creative energy, and
the sacred power resident in the past is the *source*
of that creative energy.

The various types of sacred history in the Biblical scriptures differ in essential ways from the
general dynamic of the myth just outlined,
— especially in their various relationships to
historical time, and in the personal disclosure of
God, his mind and love and will. Nevertheless, in
their own way, the sacred histories are meant to
be paradigmatic and determinative for all time.
The past in them is paradigmatic insofar as it
holds power over other times. Now a paradigmatic time is distinct from other time, for it is not
just another time; it is a holy time. Yet just in being paradigmatic it holds for these other times and
seals them with its bond, as amber catches up and
holds some latecomer in its transparent embrace.
Its efficacy as paradigm, then, demands the coincidence of its discontinuity and strangeness, on
the one hand, with its continuity and relevance,
on the other. It is paradigmatic because its absolute narrative form gives access to unqualifiedly
true existence, to absolute fullness of meaning
and power.

How a myth of origin lends itself to the later
times determines and interprets the character of

those times and manifests the inner character of
the sacred source. If we simplify and select from
the welter of various myths of origin, three modes
according to which the world comes to be are
especially significant for our purposes. They are:
by partition, emergence and intelligent activity.
First, by partition. Out of an originally indeterminate chaos a determinate order of things comes
about by a primary division (*Ur-teilen*), by differ-
entiation, discrimination, definition. The tension
in such an account is maintained by the constant
danger of losing the original unity, so that the
primary function of the myth is to recover that
unity, to sustain it and to attach its hearers to its
sacred ground. It is this threatened loss and
hoped-for recovery that Nietzsche celebrated in
the name of the Dionysian myth in his *Birth of
Tragedy*. Such a mode of creation may take one of
several forms. It may be the dismemberment of a
divine being (as Marduk kills Tiamat in *Enuma
elish*), or an original sacrifice (as that of Purusha in
Rig Veda), or the coming about of a regional division of the world (as in Hesiod where the shadowy
personifications of earthy *Gaia,* watery *Okeanos*
and airy *Uranos* fuse with their appropriate
elements and regions).[5] The ordinary analogue of
this primeval partitioning is physical division into
parts; but, as Heidegger remarks when inter-
preting the fragment of Anaximander, it expresses a pre-moral sense of rightness.[6]

The second mode of creation is that of emergence, and its ordinary analogue is growth and

development. Thus, the world develops from a
cosmic egg (in the Japanese *Nihongi,* the Chan-
dogya *Upanishad,* and a Polynesian myth); or it
emerges from mud or seed brought up out of the
deep waters (in the Amerindian Maidu or Yokuts
myths), or is ejaculated (in the Egyptian *Apophis*
myth) or vomited (in the African Bantu myth).[7]
Order here is not the distribution of ordered
parts, but rather the development of difference by
means of a spontaneity latent within an original
matter. And the tension appropriate to this account is between the original vitality and its possible wane.

The third mode of creation is that of properly
intelligent activity. By properly intelligent I mean
that creation comes about primarily through an
act of the mind or will or some other psychic
movement associated immediately and properly
with consciousness. Now the myths of partition
and emergence sometimes involve intelligent
divine beings, but the means of creation in them is
not primarily intelligent activity. In the third
mode of creation the world comes to be by
thought (in the Amerindian Winnebago myth), or
from a dream-like phantasm (in the Amerindian
Uitoto myth); or it comes about as the result of
desire (in the Hindu *Manusmriti*), or through will
(in the Zoroastrian struggle willed by *Ohrmazd*); or
it comes to be because a word is spoken (in the
Mayan *Popol Vuh,* and in a Maori myth; cf.
Genesis); or it is produced by some sort of fashioning (as in the later stages of some myths, such as

in the Zoroastrian, and especially in the making of man).[8] Plato's *Demiurge* seems to have been engaged in some sort of production, and Plato argues eloquently for the right to use technical analogies to describe the divine making (in the *Laws*).[9] Moreover, the image of the potter and the clay runs throughout the *Old* and *New Testaments*.[10] The tension in the third account of creation is between the maintenance of the invisible intention and its external realization. There may be (as in Hinduism) a call to search out the invisible intention; or corruption may threaten in the form of willed evil (as in Zoroastrianism and the Biblical religions), that is, destruction does not take the form of a reversion into primeval chaos, nor of decline into cold still death, but of an active rebellion.

The distinction of the modes of origin into partition, emergence and intelligent production is not exhaustive. Moreover, the distinction is somewhat forced, for the categories do not necessarily exclude each other completely. And finally, in any actual myth of origin there may be more than one of these modes, though one of them is dominant usually. Nevertheless, the threefold distinction draws attention to the human resources that underly most myths of origin: the experience and understanding of division, growth and decision.[11] Among the hearers of the myth, of course, there is no especial interest in these processes as such and for themselves. Indeed, excessive attention to the technical aspects tends to distract the original religious impulse, turning it towards magic and pseudo-science. These processes are religiously significant only insofar as they are the ways along which the sacred has come and comes again, and insofar as they point the way back to the sacred, so that the hearers may once again participate in the ancient power and goodness. It is not the process of origination as such that is important, but the pattern of order that results from it, and by which the hearers may conform themselves in the present and the future.

In the Greek beginnings of our own culture the transition from the cosmogonies of Hesiod and the poets to the cosmologies of Thales and the philosophers brought about a shift in the very meaning of "the beginning." For the philosophers' attention was not directed towards the beginning understood in protean fashion as a primordial past, but towards the beginning understood as first in principle and in rank (not *proto-* but *arche-*). It is not uncommon in the philosophical tradition to distinguish between questions of genesis or temporal priority, on the one hand, and, on the other, questions of nature or essence that address a priority variously described as logical or ontological. Thus, for example, in the Aristotelian analysis of substance, form has a certain priority over matter, but not a chronological priority; or again, in the Kantian analysis of cognition, the *a priori* forms have a certain priority over the *a posteriori* contents, but they are not experienced before the empirical content, the priority is not sequential. Nevertheless, the nature of that priority needs to be examined and its relation to time determined. In the shift from the primordial past of the cosmogonies to the explanatory principles of the cosmologies, is the priority a timeless one? And if it is, is it a sort of timeless past (aorist)? or simply timeless (aeontic, eternal)? Or may it be, rather, a distinctive form of the present? Does the priority have any temporal significance at all? If the quest for origin is a search for what is "first," and if the cosmogonic myths apprehend that "firstness" as a primordial past, what is "first" in the cosmological thought of the philosophers? What is philosophical "firstness"?

Within the philosophical tradition that stems from the Greeks the question of origin has received extensive and intensive consideration. At no time did it receive more consideration than in the high middle ages. Matthew of Aquasparta, a younger contemporary of St. Thomas, has left us a summary of philosophical positions on the question which he has found in the philosopher Averroes.[12] The latter had reduced the philosophical positions reached on the question to five. First, things are said to come to be through the discovery or disclosure of latent forms (attributed to Anaxagoras). Second, things may be said to come to be through the orderly arrangement of separate elements (attributed to Empedocles). Third, through the bestowal of forms (attributed to Plato and his followers). Or fourth, from a giver who is either separate from the things (attributed to

Avicenna) or somehow joined to them (attributed to Themistius). Or fifth and finally, things may be said to come to be by being lead forth from potency into act (attributed to Aristotle). None of these five positions hold that things are created from nothing, and the conclusion is that no philosopher has been able to arrive at the knowledge of creation as production from nothing, nor is one able to come to this knowledge from experience alone. If we look back over the five positions, we can see certain rough similarities with the three mythical modes of creation. The first and fifth (discovery and eduction) are not unlike emergence; the second (distribution) is not unlike partition; while the third and fourth (bestowal) are not unlike intelligent activity. Moreover, all seem to share the presupposition of a primordial state, be it chaos or matter or some other indeterminate substrate. In the above summary, then, creation is understood as a fundamental transition, a change of state; and it is interpreted by analogy with one or another basic type of change that is familiar to us from experience. Now, because all such transitions seem in fact and by necessity to require a pre-existent subject, they seem to preclude the view that creation is the production of something where there had been nothing whatever prior to creation. *Creatio de nihilo* or *ex nihilo* seems to fall outside common human experience, and consequently, outside of philosophical enquiry as such. It seems rather to belong to those theological opinions of which Descartes said that they required more than human intelligence.

Creation from nothing has been a religious and theological doctrine among Christians for centuries. Creeds and Councils of the Church have given it institutional expression. In the *Dogmatic Constitution of the Catholic Faith* decreed by the Roman Catholic bishops at the First Vatican Council (1870), it is declared in the opening chapter, entitled: "God the creator of all things," that

> in order to manifest his perfection through the benefits which he bestows on creatures — not to intensify his happiness nor to acquire any perfection — this one and only true God, by his goodness and "almighty power" and by a completely free decision, "from the very beginning of time has created both orders of creatures in the same way out of nothing, the spiritual or angelic world and the corporeal or visible universe. And afterwards he formed the creature man, who in a way belongs to both orders, as he is composed of spirit and body."

And they promulgated the associated canons, including the fifth:

> If anyone does not admit that the world and everything in it, both spiritual and material, have been produced in their entire substance by God out of nothing; or says that God did not create with a will free from all necessity, but that he created necessarily, just as he necessarily loves himself; or denies that the world was made for the glory of God: let him be anathema.[13]

The discussions at the Council on the wisdom of promulgating such a traditional dogma in these terms show that not everyone thought it prudent, and probably fewer do now. Nevertheless, there can be no doubt that this is the juridical expression of a long-standing and widespread religious belief, obtaining far beyond the communion of Roman Catholic Christians; and that it sums up the traditional strict and full belief in creation as a making out of nothing. Before we turn to examine the philosophical implications of such a notion, it is important to at least glance at the religious development of the notion, stressing certain philosophically suggestive elements, even though the resumé must remain sketchy in the extreme.

It was not unusual, even a century ago, to understand the account of creation presented in *Genesis* (1:1-2) to be the explicit affirmation of creation from nothing. Nowadays, most Biblical scholars are more reserved.[14] We are told in the Scripture that God hovered over or breathed over dark seas, a formless waste, an abyss; we are tempted to imagine formless matter. A recent literal translation puts it thus:

> When God set about to create heaven and earth—the world being then a formless waste, with darkness over the seas and only an awesome wind sweeping over the water. . . .[15]

And another, somewhat more traditionally:

> In the beginning God created the heavens and the earth. Now the earth was a formless void, there was darkness over the deep, and God's spirit hovered over the water.[16]

We ought, then, perhaps, to say initially that creation according to the Bible is some sort of production. Now there are many kinds of production. It will become clear that creation by the

Biblical God is not a mythical combat. But neither is it an emanation, such as that set forth by some Neoplatonists. Nor is it the kind of procession of which Christians speak according to which the second person of the Trinity is "begotten not made," or the third "proceeds from. . . ." Finally, creation is not a transformation, such as the self-determination of the Hegelian Absolute has sometimes been taken to be. The word used in the *Genesis* text and commonly in the Hebrew scriptures (*bārā'*: to create) denotes a special exercize of the divine power, and is attributed to God alone. Such creative action is exclusively and uniquely divine.[17]

If the explicit doctrine of creation *ex nihilo* is not to be claimed for the cosmogony set forth in *Genesis,* nevertheless it leaves no doubt about God's sovereign power and goodness; they are absolute and brook no interference. He transcends the things he has made and is utterly distinct from them. Yet his creative ordinance extends to everything, and there is no suggestion of any independent matter that escapes his creative power. It is productive, unique, universal and absolute. *Deutero-Isaiah* (44:24) expresses it forcefully:

> I myself, Yahweh, made all things, I alone spread out the heavens. When I gave the earth shape, did anyone help me?

The New Testament has numerous affirmations of such a production.[18] Among the Fathers of the Church, Clement of Rome (first century) gives beautiful voice in *The Letter to the Corinthians* to the

majestic and peaceful rule of God over history and
nature, that same rule which the Greek Fathers
celebrate in the title: *Christos Pantocrator.*

As to the manner in which creation comes
about, it is often said to be a work: God "forms,"
"fashions," "builds" and "makes"; or he "fixes"
things in their place forever. Or it comes about by
word: God "speaks" and things are done; he "commands" and things are made.[19] The *Letter to the
Hebrews* is explicit:

> It is by faith that we understand that the world was
> created by one word from God, so that no apparent cause
> can account for the things we can see. (11:3)

The emphasis upon the ease of the divine creative
work or speech is implied in the absolute sovereignty of his power, but it also sets off the creative
activity from other modes of production. Clement
of Alexandria (d. ca. 215) writes to the Greeks
that

> the sheer volition [of God] is the making of the universe.
> For God alone made it, because he alone is God in his be-
> ing. By his sheer act of will he creates; and after he has
> merely willed it, it follows that things come into being.[20]

Underlining the power and ease of the divine
work, St. Basil of Caesarea (d. 379) holds that the
work of creation was done in an instant.[21] It is
significant that in modern times the tendency has
been to interpret the "days" as long periods of
time, so as to bring the Biblical account more into
harmony with the time-scale presented by modern
scientific theory. The earlier Christians were

more concerned to bring it into harmony with
their understanding of the creative power of God.
With Athanasius (d. 373) the immediate character of creation is not only temporal; it is above all
ontological, that is, there is no intermediary.[22]
The Roman Hippolytus (d. ca. 236) understands
the divine act to be without motion;[23] and the
Greek, St. John Damascene (d. ca. 749), sum-
ming up the doctrine of creation at the end of the
Patristic period,[24] writes that a simple act of his
will suffices for this production of all things.

Creation is not a transference of being or substance to the creature at the expense of the creator, for the creator gives without diminishing his
own being. It is a work (*opus*) without toil (*labor*).
From the point of view of the effect achieved it
might be considered a transitive action, since
there result creatures which are — so to speak —
"outside" of the creator, that is, which are not the
creator, nor of his substance. But from the point
of view of the creator creation is an intransitive
activity, since creative action neither diminishes
nor augments the creator. He is neither less nor
more because he creates. There are intimations of
such power in human relationships. When we
love someone without demanding a return we do
not diminish our own being thereby. A teacher
teaches without becoming less knowledgeable; a
doctor cures without lessening his healing skill;
and an artist produces without compromising his
creative genius. But, of course, teachers grow
forgetful, physicians' hands may falter, and the

well-springs of artistic inventiveness may dry up.
And so they remain merely intimations. Creation
is an action *sui generis,* without like. St. Thomas
calls it a relation without motion:

> Creation posits something in the created thing only
> according to relation; for what is created is not made by
> motion or by change. For what is made by motion or by
> change is made from something pre-existing. . . .When
> God creates, he produces things without motion. Now
> when motion is removed from action and passion, only
> relation remains. . . .Hence creation in the creature is
> only a certain relation to the creator as to the principle of
> its being.[25]

In a study of the doctrine of creation among thirteenth century scholastic doctors, Zachary Hayes
notices that all of them are in agreement that
there is an absence of change and movement in
creation.[26] And at this point he asks:

> But the very concept of power as regards creation is prob-
> lematic. What is this power by which God creates?

That creation is the work of intelligence is implicit in the Biblical conviction that the universe is
the handiwork of God, created for his own purpose. In *Genesis* God speaks and sees, he wills and
commands, he enters into covenants with his peo-
ple, and into argument about evil and responsibility with Job. The prophets tell us that he is a loving husband, a caring father, a discerning judge.
In the Sapiential books he consorts with Wisdom.
In the Gospel and Epistles he is father of all, so
that his creative authority discloses an intelligent
care, a provident will, a benevolent purpose, a

father's love. Creation, then, is not simply a
manifest display of power; it has the interiority
appropriate to relations of intelligence. To para-
phrase St. Paul, the invisible nature of God, "his
eternal power and deity," are manifest in the visi-
ble things he has made.[27]

For all that, the creative act remains mysterious. The same Paul exclaims:

> O the depth of the riches and wisdom and knowledge of
> God! How unsearchable are his judgments and how in-
> scrutable are his ways! "For who has known the mind of
> the Lord, or who has been his counselor?" (*Is.* 40:13) "Or
> who has given a gift to him that he might be repaid?" (*Job*
> 35:7)[28]

Lactantius (d. ca. 320) protests that the failure to
comprehend the way in which creation has come
about is no good reason for denying the fact that it
has.[29] For the mystery that attaches to creation is
not a simple ignorance. It is also the very knowledge which the creature has of his own creation.
Now it is the common testimony of the Scriptures
that God has created out of his goodness and to
manifest his glory.

Out of his goodness: The philosopher-theologians
of the high middle ages, for the most part, kept
the mystery before them as they discussed the
purpose of creation. They thereby avoided that
particular anthropomorphism by which the ra-
tionalist philosophers of the seventeenth and eighteenth centuries commanded God to create only
the very best possible world that men can con-
ceive, and to do it expeditiously in the most

economical and provident way that men presently
devise.[30] St. Augustine was fond of saying that
God acts out of *his* goodness and not out of need.[31]
So that biblical creation is free not necessitated. In
contrast to some one best world, a deliberation
which is without hesitation and an intelligence
which is uncoerced is a reservoir of created goodness that includes an infinity of possiblities that
will never be realized. Hence the mystery of the
ones that are. And so, if creation is free and
deliberate, we must take the key to its meaning
not from the work realized but from that work insofar as it shows forth the mind of the creator.
Now, it is also common testimony that the goodness of the creator, out of which he creates, is the
source and term of that very goodness which the
creature is; for the goodness which the creator endows is the good of the creature. In *Deutero-Isaiah*
we read:

> I am the first and the last; there is no other God besides
> me. Who is like me? (44:6)

And in *Revelation*:

> I am the Alpha and the Omega, the Beginning and the
> End. I well give water from the well of life free to anybody
> who is thirsty. (21:6)

Deuteronomy, so famous for its binding precepts,
does not forget the divine purpose:

> And now, Israel, what does Yahweh your God ask of you?
> Only this: to fear Yahweh your God, to follow all his
> ways, to love him, to serve Yahweh your God with all

your heart and all your soul, to keep the commandments
and laws of Yahweh that *for your good* I lay down for you today. (10:12; italics added.)

St. Paul proclaims the purpose in regard to
Christians:

Before the world was made, he chose us, chose us in
Christ. . .to live through love in his presence. . .to make
us praise the glory of his grace, his free gift to us in the
beloved. . . .He has let us know the mystery of his purpose. . .which brings freedom for those whom God has
taken for his own, to make his glory praised. (*Ephes.*
1:4-14)

To manifest his glory: We are likely to feel com-
fortable with a divine goodness, but perhaps a bit
embarrassed with a divine glory. We are suspici-
ous of heroics, especially celestial ones. In an age
that has brought "public relations" to the state of a
fine art and has invented the industry of "image-
making," it is not easy to penetrate the surface
light that surrounds the word "glory" with a hard
shell.[32] Indeed, the word has all but sunk to the
derogatory meaning of "vainglory." Of course, a
vainglorious God would strike a comical and even
pathetic pose. Just because such a God would
strut before us in order to win worship from us,
we would be required to take no notice of him. To
give it and not to withhold it would be idolatry.

Now, it is just here that the modern scholarly
study of religion can help us. For it reminds us
that the "glory" of God is a theophany, the life-
giving manifestation of the sacred. It appeared to
the eyes of the sons of Israel "like a devouring fire

on the mountain top" (*Ex.* 24:16-18); but from it issued the commandments that gave life. The glory teaches Pharaoh who God is (*Ex.* 14:4, 18), and blazes out at Moses (*Ex.* 4:14). It is present in the temple where the Holy One of Israel resides (*Ex.* 40:34; 1 *Kgs.* 8:11; *Ps.* 29). It is seen to leave the Holy City (*Ezek.* 10:1-22) and to return (*Ezek.* 43:1-27). It appears as the prophesy of a judgment to come (*Dan.* 7:9), and will be revealed to all mankind (*Is.* 40:5). Jesus is transfigured by the glory (*Mt.* 17:1-8), and the disciples praise that glory (*doxa: Lk.* 19:38), returning praise for glory seen (doxology). Indeed, the incarnate Word is a continuous manifestation of the glory (*Jn.* 1:14), just as the miracle at Cana was the first of numerous intermittent signs of that glory (*Jn.* 2:11). It is the *Kabōd* of the old Testament and the *Shekhina* of Jewish traditions. It is the *doxa* of the Septuagint and the New Testament Greek which preserves the inner bond between the divine knowledge, instruction and manifestation in a way in which the Latin *gloria* (fame, reputation, honour) does not. The glory of the Biblical God, then, is what he gives of himself, that aspect of the gift that is the very presence of the giver himself. In discussing creation St. Thomas writes that God alone is the

> most perfectly liberal giver (*maxime liberalis*), because he does not act for his own profit (*utilitatem*), but only out of his own goodness.[33]

Pinard remarks that God's glorification is sufficient reason for his undertaking creation, but not

one that compelled him to it.[34] And he seems
even to suggest, with a sense of irony and drama,
that the act of creation is a grand gesture, *un geste
beau,* fully in keeping with the character of the
divine author just because it is entirely useless to
him.

The New Testament understanding of creation
is transformed by the doctrine of the *Logos* as
creative principle:

> In the beginning was the Word:/ the Word was with God/
> and the Word was God./ He was with God in the begin-
> ning./ Through him all things came to be,/ not one thing
> had its being but through him. (*Jn.* 1:1-3)[35]

The early Fathers were quick to recognize from
the form (that is, from the *incipit*: "In the beginning. . . .") and from the substance that St. John's
prologue was a creation account, a story of origins. St. Paul's preaching of the "new creation"
and the "new Adam" confirmed the eschatological
nature of the creative activity:

> He [Christ] is the image of the unseen God/ and the first-
> born of all creation,/ for in him were created/ all things in
> heaven and on earth:/ everything visible and everything
> invisible/. . .all things were created through him and for
> him./ Before anything was created, he existed/. . . .(*Col.*
> 1:15)
> And for anyone who is in Christ, there is a new creation;
> the old creation has gone, and now the new one is here. It
> is all God's work. (*2 Cor.* 5:17)
> The whole creation is eagerly waiting for God to reveal his
> sons. . .creation still retains the hope of being freed, like
> us, from its decadence, to enjoy the same freedom and
> glory as the children of God. From the beginning till now
> the entire creation, as we know, has been groaning in one
> great act of giving birth. . . .(*Rom.* 8:19-23)

> Your mind must be renewed by a spiritual revolution so
> that you can put on the new self [the new man] that has
> been created in God's way, in the goodness and holiness of
> the truth. (*Eph.* 4:24) You have put on a new self which
> will progress towards true knowledge the more it is renew-
> ed in the image of its creator. (*Col.* 1:10) The first *man,*
> Adam, as scripture says, *became a living soul;* but the last
> Adam has become a life-giving spirit. (1 *Cor.* 15:45)

And so to the goodness and glory of the first creation there is added the hope in a new creation in
goodness and glory: the kingdom that is already
at hand yet not in its fullness.

The earliest Biblical passages proclaim the absolute sovereignty of God, but without explicitly
teaching creation *ex nihilo.* No doubt the doctrine
is more than merely compatible with the Biblical
understanding of God. With the advantage of
hindsight, and given the keener recognition of the
transcendence of God, perhaps through the
experience of the exile, along with a later more
reflective and abstract cast of mind, we might
even conclude that the emergence of the conception was all but guaranteed. St. Augustine puts a
rhetorical question to the issue:

> If, then, *Genesis* is silent as to anything that God has made,
> which, however, neither sound faith nor unerring under-
> standing doubts that God has made, let not any sober
> teaching dare to say that these waters were co-eternal with
> God because we find them mentioned in the book of
> *Genesis;* but *when* they were created, we find not.
> Why — *truth instructing us* — may we not understand that
> that formless matter, which the Scripture calls the earth
> invisible and without form, and the darksome deep, have
> been made by God out of nothing, and therefore that they

are not co-eternal with him, although that narrative has
failed to tell *when* they were made? (*Conf.* 12:22; italics
added.)[36]

It has been noticed that the phrase, "out of
nothing," (*ex ouk ontōn*) occurs only late in the
Bible (2 *Maccabees* 7:28), although its context suggests a common belief. The notion of "production
out of non-being" (*ek tou me ontos*) is common
among the early Fathers of the Church. It has
been claimed that the first reasoned statement of
the doctrine is found in Clement of Alexandria (d.
ca. 215), but it seems to be common belief already
among second century Christians.[37] It is found in
Tertullian (d. ca. 220): *qui universa de nihilo produx-
erit.*[38] Gilson finds both the idea and the formula
of creation out of nothing in Theophilus, bishop
of Antioch (169). They

are there, and, for the first time, in words preclude all
hesitation on the meaning of the doctrine.[39]

Condemning the idolatrous view that the elements are divine, the apologist Aristides (fl. 117)
holds them to be assembled from nothing.[40] Ta-
tian (d. after 172) insists that matter is not without
a beginning (*anarchos*) and that the *Logos* creates
the matter he needs.[44] Theophilus warns that, if
matter were unbegotten (*agennetos*), it would be
equal to God.[42]

This theme, constantly repeated by the
Fathers, is not self-evident to us today. It could be
argued after all that an eternal matter would be
independent of God in its being, but not equal to

God in power and perfection. The underived
status of matter would be a challenge to God only
if it could claim an equal dignity with him, after
the manner of a co-eval principle. The hostility of
the early apologists and Fathers may well spring
from considerations of power and rulership rather
than from questions of being as such. The unbe-
gottenness of matter would reflect upon and compromise the absolute sovereignty of the divine
creative power, setting at least passive limits to its
exercize. It would require the divine will to rely
upon something that lay in some sense outside its
province, determining it in the way a pre-
condition functions. If such a matter could speak,
it would cry out: Without me, nothing can be
made! Moreover, there would be an aspect in
creatures themselves which they did not owe to
their God, even though that element were merely
the capacity to be formed by God. Now, it is just
such a pretention that the Fathers were determined to forestall. St. Basil protests that an underived
matter would be adorable, even as God is.[43]

On the other hand, they were equally determined to avoid an emanation that would draw
creation out of God's own substance, for then
mere creatures would be something divine.[44] En-
quiring into the origin of the possibility of human
evil, St. Augustine remarks that God does not
generate things from his own nature and substance (*de sua natura atque substantia*), but rather
makes them from nothing, precisely: from *no thing*
(de nulla re). And he adds that this does not mean

that nothing (*nihil*) has some power (*vim*), because if it did, then it would be something and not nothing.[45] A commentator[46] sums up the meaning of "from nothing" thus: "not out of God" (*non ex deo*). And he surveys the meanings of the phrase "from nothing" by rejecting two senses and accepting one. Creation does not draw upon "nothing" as from some positive matter (*non materialiter ex*), nor does it use "nothing" as an instrument (*non causaliter per*); rather, creation from "nothing" makes something to be where there was nothing before and does this by the power of the agent alone (*ordinaliter post*). So that "from nothing" indicates succession not provenance. St. Bonaventure takes "nothing" in the original rather than the material sense (*non materialiter sed originaliter*).[47]

St. Anselm of Canterbury (d. 1109) is famous for his formulation of the ontological argument, whose central conception of God is of a being than which none greater can be conceived. This God is the *creator ex nihilo*, and St. Anselm asks what the "nothing" linked with the creator can mean.[48] First, we can say of something that it is *de nihilo* and mean by this that it is not made at all; as when, — upon being asked of someone who is not actually speaking: "What did he say?" — we reply: "Nothing at all," meaning that he is not speaking. So, too, in this sense we can say that God is made *out of nothing,* because he is not *made* at all. But we cannot say this of the things that are made. Second, we can also say that something is made out of nothing, and mean by it: "not from anything."

The thing is indeed *made,* but there is *nothing from which* it is made. And in this sense we can say this of things but not of God. What must be rejected, however, is a third sense which construes "nothing" as a sort of "something existent" out of which a thing is able to come into being. Now this rejected interpretation is not unlike the mythical presupposition of primeval chaos and not unlike the material substrate that underlies the five positions summed up by Matthew of Aquasparta from Averroes. So that the long Christian reflection upon the term: *creatio ex nihilo* does not fly in the face of the ancient Greek axiom: from nothing nothing comes.[49] Rather, it forces a distinction in the preposition "from" (*de*) or "out of" (*ek, ex*), a distinction between an efficient or productive causality and a material causality. Creation comes *from* God by way of agency, but the divine production is *from nothing* by way of material causality, i.e., it issues from no material substrate.

So far St. Anselm's reflection is admirable in its precision and piquant in its linguistic approach, but then something even more intriguing occurs in his metaphysics. After having just taken up the sense of the term, "from nothing," he passes to the category of gift. I myself had come to appreciate the importance of this category by another route, namely, by way of anthropology; and to this I will shortly return. But it is important first to hear the metaphysician, and then to carry his argument further perhaps than he has:

We can say suitably and without any inconsistency that those things which have been made by the Creative Substance were made from nothing — in the way that we commonly say that a rich man has been made from a poor man (*ex paupere*) or that from sickness (*ex aegritudine*) a man has regained (*recepisse*) health. That is, he who was previously poor is now rich — something that he was not beforehand; and he who previously was sick now has health — something which he did not have beforehand. In this manner, then, we can fittingly understand the following statements: "The Creative Being has made all things from nothing" and "Through the Creative Being all things have been made from nothing" — that is, things that once were nothing are now something. . . .Thus, when we observe a man of meager means who has been elevated by a second man to great wealth or honor, we say, "The second man has made the first man from nothing."[50]

Making is to be understood as an endowment, an elevation to a certain status; by analogy, creation is a donation from nothing. What is especially keen about St. Anselm's turn of thought is his appeal to the concept of privation as a way of understanding the "nothing." The accepted technical sense of the term "privation" was derived from the Aristotelian analysis of accidental change.[51] The factors functional in accidental change, according to this analysis, are (1) a subject underlying the change (substance), (2) a form acquired or lost through the change (accident), and (3) the lack of that form at the beginning or end of the change (privation). In such a dynamism the privation is bound into a relation of contrariety with its appropriate form, on the one hand, and, on the other, into a relation of inherence in its proper subject. In sum, privation is the lack of a good appropriate to a definite subject (*tóde ti,* this something of a certain kind). It is the specific absence of a due good, either as a lack not yet filled, or as a good that has been lost (in which event it is an evil). In turning to the more basic kind of change, however, that is, to substantial generation and corruption, Aristotle could find no role for privation.[52] This was because he refused to attribute a specific lack to the pure indeterminate potency of primary matter which underlay the substantial change and which, for him, was an ultimate principle. Since it possessed no determinate character, it could not suffer a specific lack.

For St. Anselm the horizon has widened and deepened. In using the concept of privation to interpret creation *de nihilo* he has given to the concept an absolute sense. A certain ambiguity haunts the more ordinary meaning of the term (*privo, steréo*: to take away, rob; *privatio, stéresis*: loss). It can mean deprivation, the more or less violent loss of a good once possessed; or it can mean the milder absence of a good expected to be present. Both the loss and the absence are founded upon a certain expectation, a sort of claim that arises from the nature of the subject of the privation, the thing. If we speak of an absolute privation, on the other hand, there can be no subject. There can be nothing due or owing, there can be nothing expected or anticipated, because there is no subject to which to refer the dueness, no subject to give rise to the expectation. And so, the ful-

filment of the absent good is absolutely gratuitous, is strictly speaking: not called for. Now, it is
in this sense that St. Anselm exploits the meaning
of the term in his analogy, so that it is freed from
its entrenchment with a contrary form and a
definite subject. It is freed from the specificity that
gave rise to the expectations ingredient in the ordinary sense of the term. In the Anselmian
analogy, the privation indicates no determinate
lack rooted in a specific subject, because there is
no subject at all.

The term denotes *after the fact* the state of affairs
before the endowment. It makes no strict sense to
say, before I have received a gift, that I am giftless
as though there is a lack in me in the way that a
painting lacks the right colour, a horse has
become lame, or a student is yet to learn geo-
metry. Certainly, before I have received a gift, I
am without a gift; I simply do not have one. But I
do not lack something due me. And yet, viewed
after the fact, after the endowment, the lack of
that endowment is more than a simple negation.
By a "simple negation" I mean such denials as,
that "apples are not oranges," or that "stones don't
speak." We might call these latter, "absolute"
negations. They are dead-end, leading nowhere
beyond themselves. Apples simply are not
oranges, and that is that; and stones simply don't
speak, nor should we expect them to. Yet the lack
of the gift in one who is giftless, seen in retrospect,
after the giving, is more than an absolute negation
that leads nowhere. It is, rather, an absolute pri-

vation, that in retrospect does lead somewhere.
For once the good has been given and received, it
is accepted as appropriate to the recipient. The
riches were not due the poor man; otherwise they
would be repayment in justice, not endowment in
generosity. They are appropriate to him, nevertheless, and the giving is appropriate. We have
more here than a simple negation, but we have it
only after the fact, not before. The gift is not as
such a remedy for some lack, but is rather an
unexpected surplus that comes without prior conditions set by the recipient. The element of gratuity indicates that there is no ground in the recipient for this gift, so that the gift is strictly uncalled
for. It is not compensation for something previously done, though it may be given in gratitude.
Nor is it commiseration for something that ought
to be present, though it may be given out of
mercy. Creation is to be understood as the reception of a good not due in any way, so that there
cannot be even a subject of that reception. It is absolute reception; there is not something which
receives, but rather sheer receiving. Before the
endowment, there is nothing; after the reception,
we can in retrospect speak of the prior state as an
absolute privation, that is, a privation which
(unlike an absolute negation) has led somewhere.
But where? The absolute privation points back to
a negation that is neither an unfulfilled potentiality in the capacity of a recipient, nor a loss suffered
by the recipient, nor a negation that is simply indifferent in regard to him. It is a distinctive state

that must be traced back, not to the recipient at
all, but to the donor, to the giver rather than the
receiver.[53] Strictly speaking, creation is not an affair of the creature, except after the fact; but that
"after the fact" is, as we shall see, everything for
the creature.

II

Studies in anthropology over the past century
have made available to us an understanding of the
meaning of the gift in pre-literate societies. That
meaning is still significant for us today, because in
its deepest and broadest import it still is capable of
functioning in modern life. The prevailing attitude, however, is not favorable to the extension of
the category of the gift beyond situations limited
to interaction between humans. Giving and receiving is taken to be an affair between humans,
except where sentiment extends it to our pets. An
older wisdom spoke of "the gifts of Mother Earth,"
of "gifts from the gods," and of "the gift of life."
But such locutions are not easily understood today, and they are likely to be sloughed off as
poetic imagery and archaic metaphor. To be sure,
religious sciptures may sometimes speak this way
and find their voice in religious hymns; but what
in them is decorous imagery and what is reality?
The chief obstacle to a better appreciation of the
category of the gift is a widespread current attitude towards the world; it is the attitude that takes
the world as a *given fact*. Now these two words

need looking into, for their joint meaning is not obvious, and there is nothing direct or simple about their common usage. They are a way of understanding what is before us, around us, present to us. They are burnt deeply into the outlook of the so-called "advanced" societies. They provide a primary interpretation of what is evident. They combine to form the first name we give to what we encounter. Moreover, in scientific and learned discourse and in everyday speech as well, this initial name proves ultimately decisive and presides over most subsequent understanding of the world, so that our thought seldom breaks free from this first determination of the things that are.

We say of something that it is "there." But what do we mean when we say that it is "given?" Do we not say more than that it is simply there? Do we not add something? Do we not add a fundamental attitude towards what is there? The nomenclature and the usage express the attitude. Current English[54] usage draws a sharp distinction between most uses of "the given" and "the gift"; and not only English: — French distinguishes *la donnée* from *le don;* and Latin harbours a distinction between *datum* and *donum.* The first members of these pairs (*given, donnée, datum*) usually serve a learned function in the discourse of the natural and positive sciences and in empiricist philosophy, often in the Latin plural form, *data.* Indeed, much of the usage comes into English from the technical vocabulary of late medieval Latin, though it is nowadays widely used in technology

and in more or less educated popular speech as
well. *The given (data)* has two meanings which are
distinct and yet compatible with one another.
There is first its hypothetical meaning which has
arisen in highly conditioned contexts: — in logic,
where it is used to designate the basis for an argument, hence: "The premisses being given, it follows that. . . ."; in mathematics, where it assigns a
non-problematic status to a postulate for the sake
of a demonstration, hence: "Granted that. . . .";
and in navigation, where it denotes the basis for
the construction of a position from which a course
can be devised. The generic meaning of these is
that of "granting, positing, conceding" some item,
so that further argument or construction can
follow upon it as from a basis and starting-point.
It designates what Hegel called a "foundation"
(*Grundlage*) rather than a "source" (*Grund*). The
term "given" expresses some agreement, provi-
sional or otherwise, among the parties relevant to
the operation or discourse which is to follow upon
the concession. In this its concessive or hypothetical sense, it serves as an agreed upon stipula-
tion, expressed by the term: "If we grant that. . . ."

But there is a second sense: the evidential
meaning of the term. Something is said to be *given*
if it is taken to be the direct yet warranted observation of what is actually the case. The connec-
tion between the hypothetical and the evidential
meanings seems to be the conviction that what is
evident is both the case and also what every
"right-thinking" observer agrees is the case. So

that the term: "Given that. . ." refers as much to the thinker addressed as to the matter designated. Moreover, what the evidential and the hypothetical sense share is that both are taken as the basis and starting-point for some sort of progression, either in discourse (an argument) or in actuality (a construction or production). *The given* is taken to be the starting-point for scientific discourse, for technological advance, and for more general forms of progressive action. *The given* is accepted for the sake of the use that can be made of it as a starting-point. The cast of mind is towards future development and results.

A combination of pressures in modern scientific discourse has produced what at first seems to be a paradoxical usage. The characterization of what is there as *given* is meant to rigorously exclude any reference to a giver; hence the expression: "It is simply given." This closure on itself is mirrored in the etymology of the term. Thus, in the Latin from which the usage takes it origin, the term for gift (*donum*) is a direct extension of the verbal stem (*do*, give), whereas the term for the given (*datum*) is formed from the past participle and thereby suggests a finished state, completed within itself. An epistemology that limits itself to *data* does not permit the knower to go "behind" or "beneath" *the given* in search of an ontological cause. The only justifiable reason for returning to *the given* is in order to reconfirm the basis of the progression, to re-examine the argument at its starting-point, to repeat the experiment from the first step onward, or to refine the method of production: in a word, to verify the development and the result. If the initial *given* is broken down by analysis, a new *given* appears; but *givenness,* that is, the characterization of the evidence as given, does not disappear. The "fact of having been given" monitors the progression. Thus, physics starts with corpuscles, and then passes on the molecules, to atoms, to protons and so on; but each new temporary point of rest is itself characterized as a *given*. Nor is there any talk of a giver. No doubt this usage reflects a combination of factors in modern discourse: the constructivist temper brought about through the mathematical and experimental tendencies in modern science, the exigency for application animating scientific technology, and the positivist temper of philosophers influenced by these factors, such as Hume, Kant and others. The givenness of the given remains inviolate in such discourse, and admits of no giver within its semantic field. In its hypothetical as well as its evidential sense the term enjoys a certain absolution from the conditions of explanation and inference just because it lies prior to them as their starting-point; it stands free from and prior to them just insofar as it is first. This structure of discourse — empiricist and phenomenalist — has been challenged recently. I do not think that the controversy of sense-data altered very much, however, since its challenge was directed primarily towards the absurdities of interposing *sensa* between knowers and the world, while it left intact the structure of givenness. No doubt the linguistic turn taken by the so-called ordinary language philosophers drew attention away from *data* to agents, as when Austin drew attention to performatives and speech acts. But the more long-range critique has been mounted by the work of hermeneutics in the social and humanistic fields; for it restricts the *given* to the natural sciences and characterizes its own evidence in other ways.[55] Nevertheless, even here the turn is not to a giver in the traditional sense. Moreover, the characterization of the evidence as *given* still determines a wide range of conventional understandings.

Turning to the semantics of the term "fact," we are familiar with the phrase: "Given the fact that. . ." which couples the two terms together. Here the term "given" in its combined evidential and hypothetical sense is reinforced by the term "fact" in its evidential sense. "It is a fact that. . ." is equivalent to "It is actually the case that. . . ," and to "It is a matter of fact that. . . ." This evidential sense is the common current meaning:

> Something that has really occurred or is actually the case; something certainly known to be of this character; hence, a particular truth known by actual observation or authentic testimony, as opposed to what is merely inferred, or to a conjecture or fiction; a datum of experience, as distinguished from the conclusions that may be based upon it.[56]

There are nuances in this dictionary account. The term designates a real occurrence ("actually the case"); it is "a datum of experience;" and it is what is "certainly known." This complex meaning of

fact has been shaped within the problematic of
human cognition, with attention to how realities
can be known. It points, therefore, not only to the
matter of evidence, to what is there, but also to
the human conditions required to certify it. Hence
the authority of the phrase: "It is a fact that. . ." or
"It is a known fact that. . . ." Uncontroverted facts
are few, however, and the term has been sub-
jected to more and more analysis by theoretically
inclined historians, for whom an historical fact is
not simply what is there in the evidence, but
rather the product of a long process of selection
and discrimination that, along with what is there,
includes also the interests of the historian, the pro-
fessional standards of the historical guild, the
availability of testimony, the canons of argumen-
tation, the demands of systematic coherence and
the spirit of the times. The use of the term "fact" in
history is a methodical disciplined use that draws
upon an older sense of the term, according to
which a fact is not simply what is there, but is
rather something that is somehow fashioned or
made (from the Latin: *facio:* do, make). The
somewhat archaic "feat" means "a thing done"
(from the Old French: *fait*). In sum, then, the
term "fact" has for its foreground, focus and surface what is actually the case, the evidence; but
that evidence comes forward from a background
of selective attention guided by an implicit understanding of what is significant for a distinctive
kind of discourse. To speak of what is there as
given fact is to speak within the circle of a discourse

that directs attention to the matter insofar as the matter is capable of satisfying certain conditions that are determinded *a priori* and in accordance with the demands of objective method; that is, the matter must satisfy the set of conditions by which the evidence can be presented in the form of objects standing over against the human knower and in a state of mutual exclusion. This objective sense of the evidence produces the domain in which the *given fact* is primary. It is important to acknowledge the remarkable results achieved in this way in the natural sciences, and also in some aspects of the human and social sciences. But it needs to be said that such a domain of discourse is not the only domain; and that such a mode of discourse closes out the more primitive semantic atmosphere that arises before us as we reflect upon the gift rather than upon the given.

At the beginning of the nineteenth century a radical shift from the empiricist-phenomenalist epistemology brought with it a drastic revision in the meaning of evidence. Thus, according to Hegel, nothing is simply given; everything is the result of a *self-giving* carried through from first to last by Absolute Spirit (*Geist*). In this sense, everything is *self-given*. The anthropocentric turn taken immediately after Hegel by Feuerbach, Marx and others gave rise to humanisms in which the *self* at the root of the *self-given* was humanity itself, either as a totality (mankind) or as a part (a nation, or a class, or especially significant individuals). Liberal belief in progress and socialist faith in

revolutionary *praxis* could both become humanist
ideals once it was assumed that the existing social
order has been brought about *solely* by the same sort
of agency as modern men possess; so that what has
been made by that agency alone is able to be im-
proved upon or destroyed and remade by it
alone.[57] This is the prinicple of human autonomy
that is shared by liberal and revolutionary ideolo-
gies alike. Their differences are important, to be
sure; for they disagree about the type of man who
will be the agent for all of mankind, and they disagree over what means are to be used to accomplish
the goal. Nevertheless, in at least one important
aspect, they share a trait already present in the
earlier sense of the *given;* for the cast of mind is still
emphatically oriented towards the future, towards
strictly human possibilities and towards means
with which man is fully competent. The absolute
release of *the given* that characterizes the earlier
outlook ("Simply given") has been transferred to the
absolute power of the transforming agency ("man
alone"). This is the root of the justification of the
claims made for both liberal progress and revolutionary action. But although these two anthropo-
morphic forms of self-givenness are the most effective today, Hegel has put the issue of self-givenness
with greater power and comprehension; for in addition to the secular sphere which includes human
discourse and action along with natural processes,
he has claimed to sublate into a single all-
embracing process of self-activity the religious
sphere of divine action and discourse as well.

We might ask whether such self-activity ought to be characterized as self-giving? It seems that the terms "self-giving" and "self-given" are somewhat forced. Perhaps that is why many of us react with misgiving when an advertiser urges us "to give yourself the best," by which is meant: "Buy something you don't really need." But after all of the word-magic is over, buying is simply not giving, nor is taking possession receiving. Perhaps the huckster is counting on an old amalgam of greed and the attractiveness of giving and receiving. The magic spell is broken once we realize that we can't really *give* anything to ourselves. If the gift we receive is wholly at our command and within our power, it is not in any strict sense a gift. In his analysis of desire Hegel insists that the self and not the object desired is the primary term of desire, so that all desire is desire of self, precisely, the self as satisfied.[58] And he characterizes self-desire and the activity which strives for self-satisfaction as a struggle to take possession of another. In his general articulation of the process of absolute self-determination he does not characterize it as a "self-giving," but appeals to other categories of action, viz., to positing, self-causation and self-determination. Through these categories he seeks to bring to discourse the movement of reality understood as a process of absolute self-determination, and to express that process as a fully coherent and adequate system of conceptual knowledge.[59] Now to talk the language of self-determination is not to talk the language of gift, for to give a gift properly speaking is neither to posit oneself nor to determine oneself in the articulation of a system; it is to embark upon an originative activity that is radically non-systematic.

A reflective understanding of the *gift* is available to us in the empirical studies carried out over the past century by anthropologists, sociologists and historians of religion.[60] But it is also as near to us as our experience of generosity in others and ourselves. I have suggested that the semantic energy of such generosity is quite unlike the relatively unbroken formal necessity to which the empirio-mathematical and systematic sciences aspire on the basis of the *given* or by way of self-determination. For the term *gift* is rooted in a domain of significance that is charged with discontinuity and contingency, with risk, vulnerability and surprise. Moreover, the gift points beyond itself to its source, to a more or less definitely apprehended giver.

What is a gift? It is a free endowment upon another who receives it freely; so that the first mark of a gift is its gratuity. Even the banal conventional acceptance, — "Oh! but you shouldn't have; it really wasn't necessary!" — expresses this inherent gratuity. There is a quality of absoluteness about a gift in the fullest sense. I have already remarked upon the absoluteness or unconditionality that attaches to the given, viz. its incontrovertibility either by supposition (the hypothetical sense) or in fact (the evidential sense). There is also a kind of absoluteness that is endemic to the process of self-determination according to Hegel (Absolute Spirit) and his successors ("man alone"). The character which the unconditional takes in the gift, however, is just its gratuity. Of course, we ought not to expect to find in the concrete and actual human situation pure interactions of giving and receiving unmixed with other qualities and intentions. The line between a gift and a transaction, a piece of business, is eidetically clear enough, but it is not always clear in life itself, nor should we expect it to be. We know of societies in which a return gift is expected, and whose nature is precisely defined, its value weighed and ranked. Is such a handing over a *gift*? Or is it an exchange of "presents" undertaken out of social duty, for social advantage, or even as part of a commercial transaction? If something is given out of gratitude, it is caught in the temper of the gift; but if it is in "compensation" for something received or expected, then it falls away from the character of the gift towards that of a transaction. Now a commercial transaction (whether in monetary or other value) is an exchange measured in terms of some standard of merit (*mereo, merx, commercium*), whereas a gift is in the strict sense unmerited. A gift, then, *qua* gift does not call for an "adequate return" upon the endowment; such a return is appropriate to investments of a commercial sort. There certainly are mixed donations, most obviously in societies where custom is formalized. We have often given a "gift" because it was expected. There is, of course, nothing wrong in this, and such interpersonal and social interaction makes affairs run more easily; not without danger, however, as shown by the ease with which innocent "gifts" imperceptibly move along a line towards bribery and coercion. Still, external forms of interaction, however empty and shallow they may at times become, remind us of an essential generosity without which life itself dies. In some situations a gift may be expected and be very precisely defined, in an other it may be expected but not so exactly defined, in an other it may not be expected at all, and in still an other it may be unexpected. The two latter unobligatory situations approach most closely the full nature of the gift, whereas the former two might better be called (as I have just suggested) "presents." Although such presents may be all but obligatory, they may still be beneficial, for not all human relationships take the form of giving and receiving. Nevertheless, the more or less obligatory situations do not realize the fullest possibility of the gift. Sometimes the routine manner of accepting presents — even with a ritual "surprise" built in — testifies to the diminution of that possibility. If presents in such situations do take on the genuine aura of the gift, it will be because the one who presents them has invested them with personal attentiveness beyond what is called for by the formal exchange of presents. Not satisfied with discharging the minimal conditions of the exchange, he or she will have seized its deeper possibility, endowed the presentation with his or her own care, and thereby transformed a mere present into a genuine gift. Such a giver will have made more than a presentation; he will have made a present into a gift. Now, the "extra" beyond the mere present is the gratuity that animates the gift. So far, then, we have recognized the non-obligatory character of the gift.

Despite the absolute gratuity inherent in the gift as endowment, reciprocity is appropriate to the gift. A gift is meant to be reciprocated. The fundamental reciprocity called for, however, is not the return of another gift. It is rather the completion of the gift being given. Now, for its completion a gift must not only be offered; it must also be received. So that reception is the original reciprocity intended in the very meaning and reality of the gift. Receptivity on the part of the recipient is the primary requisite for the completion of the gift. But the appropriate kind of receptivity is not that of passive inertia. Gabriel Marcel has distinguished between passivity and receptivity.[61] The wax undergoes the imprint of the mold and may be said to "receive" it; but such passivity is especially characteristic of physical matter. A truly human mode of receptivity calls for the recipient to rally his human resources in order to make a good reception. For example, when we receive a guest into our home, we are attentive to his needs, so that we might make him "feel at home." Now, it is just such attentive receptivity that is called for by a gift. To accept it absent-mindedly, with indifference or even hostility, would not really be to receive it at all. The gratuity inherent in the gift, moreover, requires that the receptivity be grounded in what Marcel called "availability" (*disponibilité*), the ontological disposition in which we are ready to accept the unexpected, to make room for it.[62] The reception of the gift does not follow from the endowment in the manner of a secure formal inference, but is broken by the radical surprise occasioned by the gratuity at the source of the gift. The primary reciprocation, therefore, is the acknowledgement of that gratuity and the appropriation of the gift as gratuitously given. But, if the gratuity is to be maintained, the reception must be free. In the degree to which the recipient is free in regard to the endowment, in that degree he is able to make an appropriate response. And if he is not free. . . ? Was it not Charles Peguy who prayed to God that the poor might forgive us the bread we give them? The gratuitous character (*gratuitus*) of the endowment must also animate its reception (*gratitudo*). Such receptivity is needed to bring the gift to completion. Endowment, then, does not alone realize the gift; gratitude is also called for.[63]

It follows that, in giving and receiving, there is risk for both the giver and the receiver. It may go badly. For the recipient, because the giver may seek to entrap the receiver by his gift, thus abusing the gift. For the donor, because the receiver may repel the advance made by the giver with his gift, thus abusing the generosity. Again, there is risk for the giver: for his gift may be refused, and

there is something marred about a gift that is badly received, — either accepted gracelessly, or rejected outright. Such a refusal is the original form
of non-reciprocity that preys upon and spoils a
gift, rendering it not only uncompleted but flawed
as well. For when it is refused, a gift, so to speak,
bends back upon the giver, leaving him exposed
and wounded. In an intimate relationship the
refusal is felt as a personal rebuff; in a more public
relationship it is likely to become an occasion for
uninvited shame. The wound is not only to the
dignity of the giver, however, who may be able to
tolerate it. More importantly, it may be an of-
fence against the very spirit of generosity itself,
cutting off its out-reach. But there is risk to the
receiver as well, who is made vulnerable by the
initiative of the giver. Risk attaches to reception
differently than to endowment. In reception the
receiver opens himself up to the intention of the
giver and to the significance of the gift. If giving
and receiving are stabilized by customary forms
in a society, the essential quality of the gift may be
lost for both giver and recipient by virtue of the
automatism lurking in such forms. But in a less
formal society it may also not be easy to give and
to receive a gift appropriately. If no relationship
exists between the two parties, the gift is meant to
establish one; and if a relationship already exists,
it may alter that relationship. So that both parties
are put at risk in giving and receiving.

Then, too, there may be an opacity about the
gift that creates a certain ambiguity. This is

especially true if the gift has its own material
value. For a material thing is not transparent; it is
opaque, and that opacity may hide as much or
more than it reveals of the intentions of the giver.
Its independent substance may contain an unforeseen chain of possible consequents. Long after the
gift has been given and accepted, it may subsist as
a pledge of fidelity or, if dispositions or circum-
stances alter, as an encumbrance or an embarrassment. Moreover, the material or symbolic
value of a gift may distort a relationship, its
"weight" unbalancing the relationship or prevent-
ing a promising development. And so the risk is
rooted not only in the dispositions of the donor
and the recipient, but in the opacity of the gift
itself. So far, then, we have seen: (1) the gratuity
inseparable from the gift as such, (2) the primary
reciprocity that brings the gift to completion: gratitude as the free reception of the gift, and (3) the
risk inherent in the vulnerability of the parties and
the opacity of the gift.

Just as the original gift may hide the intentions
of the giver and hold within it unforeseen conse-
quences, so too a return gift may be opaque. To
be sure, it may embody a more or less genuine,
even innocent, gratitude, a non-devious show of
appreciation, just as the original gift may be a
sign of genuine affection. On the other hand, the
return may be an attempt to forestall the original
gift in order to reject it in its givenness, to cancel
out its having been given. The return may intend
to reduce the original gift to a mere present, and

to "pay off" the "indebtedness" incurred by the reception of the original gift. In this way, the return may be meant to discharge a social obligation and to announce a newly regained freedom from such a debt. And so a return gift may actually embody the outright refusal to accept the original gift, representing the refusal to be obligated, rather than the acceptance of mutual obligations. If not outright refusal, at the very least a gift returned with such intent signifies a grudging acceptance of the original gift. Such an unfree reception expresses the very opposite disposition to gratitude, since to be grateful is to accept something unmerited (*gratia,* grace) willingly and gladly. On the other hand, many concrete situations remain obscure, even to the parties involved. The ambiguity in an interchange of gifts may remain until some unequivocal act of generosity breaks through and declares the inherently free character of giving and receiving, or until an equally unequivocal act announces by a negative freedom the deliberate refusal to take up the relationship intended by the gift. It is important to remember that there is nothing wrong with the interchange of presents out of mixed motives, for such exchange may well make smooth the pathways of interpersonal, social and even commercial relations. Moreover, not all gifts have to be accepted, anymore than they have to be given. But, if a gift is to reach its maturity, true to type, then it needs to be received with gratitude and not compensated for by a return gift.

handwritten annotations: —Acceptance ⎤⎫ response to free gift —Gratitude ⎦⎭

For all that has just been said, nothing is more customary, of course, than the exchange of gifts. We are told that pre-literate men hastened to return another gift in order to re-establish the equilibrium unbalanced by the initial gift;[64] and this reaction is not unknown among us today. Once again, a return gift is not by its very nature a refusal or non-acceptance; but it is important to recognize that the gift is not *first* completed by the return of another gift. For a new gift introduces a fresh act of giving into the relationship. And so it is strictly not a *return* gift, but a new initiative. To be sure, a return gift is founded upon the reception of the first gift, and so it might be called a gift in return. Indeed, the gratitude with which a genuine gift is properly received itself founds an intentionality that seeks expression. The expression may surface in words and facial expressions, or in gestures or conduct. But it often tends to take tangible form in the offering of a gift in return. What finds expression in such exchange at its best is the mutual affection and respect within which both parties are at once receivers and givers to each other. It is in this way that mutual gifts build community by a cumulative effect. For, as Van der Leeuw has insisted, the *do ut des* formula associated with religious offerings to the gods is not to be taken as a contractual *quid pro quo,* but rather in the diffuse creative sense that "I give in order that you might be able to give."[65] So that, although the original gift cannot be returned, it can make possible a gift in return. This bond of

affection and respect rests upon the original receptivity of giving and receiving. Once again, in the
concrete building of community the mutual interchange arises out of a mixture of motives; but the
quality of the community is determined in a significant way by the degree to which the exchange
participates in the inherent generosity of the gift.

When we examine the gift within the concrete
milieu of human life, several features are suggestive. First, if we look back over our own lives, and
then still farther back through the long career of
human existence, we find a disparity between
donors and recipients, an inequity and non-
equivalence. This non-convertibility is channelled
into various traditions: religious, artistic, political, familial, scientific, technical, and others.
Now a tradition is a chain of benefactors who pass
on or hand over human goods (*trado,* give over).
Such is the concrete human condition that the
motives are usually mixed and often obscure, and
that the goods are beset with imperfection or
worse. Nevertheless, a tradition is a benefaction,
and the donors stand in a non-reciprocal relation
to the recipients. In regard to most benefactors in
this temporal chain, the only way in which the
recipients can reciprocate is by receiving the
benefits well. Thus, for example, I cannot "repay"
Plato or Aristotle or St. Thomas, except by receiving their words thoughtfully, that is, by subjecting
them to serious critical attention. It is obvious
that time makes any other reciprocity impossible.
We remember teachers, too, whom we can never

"repay" except by trying to teach others. Reciprocity is called for as in the reception of every gift;
but a straightforward reciprocal relation is impossible. We need now to consider the nature of
that impossiblity and the reason for it.

In the atmosphere of freedom that animates the
gift as such we have recognized a necessity that is
consonant with the gratuity of the gift. It is, of
course, a necessity that is radically other than the
determinism which opposes indeterminism in
physical interaction. This necessity is the original
reciprocity that calls for the appropriate reception
of the gift in order to bring the gratuitous initiative to completion. We have also recognized the
original non-reciprocity that consists of the refusal
of the gift. And finally, we have recognized the
possibility, even the likelihood, of a founded reciprocity that incarnates itself in offering a gift in
return, thereby giving expression and embodi-
ment to the original receptivity in and through a
mutual exchange of gifts among co-existent members of a community. The impossibility of reciprocation that we are presently considering is, however, none of these. It is rooted in the disparity
between donor and recipient. Moreover, the inequity which founds the impossiblity of recipro-
cating in relation to past benefactors is not simply
due to the irreversibility of time. Even when my
father was alive, I could not return a *father's* love to
him, except by receiving it as his son and by loving my children with a love not unlike his. And so
the non-reciprocality is rooted, not simply in the

temporal condition of the giver, but in his ontological status *qua* donor; and also in the character
of the giver (whether a father or an inventor,
etc.), in the nature of the gift (whether life or a
technique, etc.), and in the actuality and uniqueness of the concrete relationships. The last feature
is decisive. A tradition is a chain of *actual* benefac-
tions. It is not parentage-in-general that gives life,
or technical insight that invents a tool; rather, it is
this giver and *that* receiver. The inequity inherent
in the gift is rooted in an actual initiative from
which the gift issues. Giving and receiving is an
existential relation and issues from a unique actuality: *this* giver, either an individual, a pair or a
group. The recipient may become a giver in turn
and assume membership in a tradition; but the
first giver and the gift remain unique, so that *that*
gift can never simply be "repaid" to the donor or
donors in the way that accounts are settled.

After insisting upon the uniqueness of the
giver, be the donor one or many, it seems paradoxical to insist also that most of them remain
anonymous to their recipients. But the uniqueness of the giver, that is, that he or they be actually existent individuals or groups, is an ontological
condition, required by the actual relationship of
endowment that constitutes giving and receiving;
whereas the anonymity of most donors to their recipients is an epistemological condition. We recognize a certain diffuseness with respect to those
to whom we owe the goods we enjoy. Thousands
of unasked for favours have been strewn through

my life, and even more have gone unnoticed or
unknown by me. I cannot make use of the sim-
plest technique which did not have to be dis-
covered and brought to excellence by nameless
craftsmen; so that most of my benefactors remain
unknown to me. Some of us can name a few gene-
rations of our ancestors, but before long the chain
of those who have helped to give us life fades away
into obscurity. Such anonymity is constitutive of
human life as we know it. The second suggestive
feature of the concrete milieu of giving and receiving, then, is the epistemological anonymity of
most donors.

The non-reciprocation by recipients to unique
but anonymous donors is inextricable from
human life and human society. The third suggestive feature of giving and receiving, then, is precisely the one that offended the young Sartre, viz.,
what he called the "excess" of existence in contrast
to the clean outline of thought.[66] An appreciation
of the gift, however, welcomes it as unmerited
abundance. If human life is impossible without
the web of non-reciprocal, unique but mostly
anonymous giving and receiving, then the gift
communicates the indispensable generosity of life
itself. There is, then, in any particular gift, not
only its special character, but also a certain transcendental character by which it bears a universal
good and releases the generosity without which
life is impossible. This transcendental character is
inseparable from every genuine gift and is constitutive of man and his world. "It is the nature of

the good to spread and communicate itself," wrote St. Thomas, citing the Dionysian refrain: *bonum diffusivum sui.* [67] The transcendental generosity calls for a transcendental receptivity, availability and openness.

The foregoing reflection has uncovered the following features of the gift: (1) the gratuity of the gift; (2) the act of endowment by the giver; (3) the original reciprocity: the reception or refusal; (4) the mutual risk to both parties; (5) the additional risk because of the material or symbolic opacity of most gifts; (6) the community built up through the exchange founded upon the original giving and receiving; (7) the non-parity of the parties and the consequent non-reciprocation; (8) the uniqueness and actuality of the relation and the parties; (9) the anonymity of most donors; and (10) the transcendental aspect of the generosity that spreads a sort of diffusive goodness throughout the situation.

In barest outline the simple situation in which a gift is given and received contains three ontological elements, — the giver, the gift and the receiver:

$$g - sg - r.$$

Something is given (sg) by someone (g) to someone else (r), even while that something (sg) is received by someone (r) from someone else (g). A gift is often thought of merely as something that passes from the ownership of one person into the possession of another. Certainly, we cannot give what is not ours to give. But the pleasure, surprise, and sometimes the solemnity, embarrassment, or uneasiness that attends the reception of a gift points to a deeper flow of energy. We transfer money from one account to another, and furniture from one house to another; but something more moves with a gift. An act of giving initiates a movement that leaves things different than they were. The act is critical in that is divides what has been from what is and will be. It is a crisis (*krino, cerno:* separate; *krisis:* decision, issue). It involves giver and receiver in a relationship that has been newly established by the act or in a relationship that has been modified by it. A gift may be more or less meaningful, of course, but its meaning as gift does not derive primarily from its subsistent value, that is, from its independence outside of or apart from the context in which it serves as gift. That is why the widow's mite may be a greater gift than a king's ransom. Inasmuch as it is a gift, it draws the giver as well as the receiver into the relationship. It presents the giver to the receiver. In that presentation the thing acquires an "inside." Now, the "outside" is the independence of the thing given, considered apart from the relationship; and in this exteriority lies it opacity. But the "inside" is the interior bond by which the giver commends himself to the receiver. The lower limit at which something ceases to be a gift is that limit at which all interiority fails, that is, where no giver is present. To an uninvolved spectator a gift might seem to detach itself from one possessor to pass over into the possession of another. But that is to observe only the physics of transference that sometimes accompanies a gift; it is not to grasp the metaphysics of the gift itself. The giver does not hand over something "outside" of himself but under his control; rather, he builds up the thing into a gift by loaning it his own conscious intention as he attends to the receiver. In the act of endowment the giver makes himself present to the receiver; and in this attentive presence he does not only give what is his, he commends himself. In his essay entitled "gifts," Emerson writes:

> The only gift is a portion of thyself. Thou must bleed for me. Therefore the poet brings his poem; the shepherd, his lamb; the farmer, corn; the miner, a gem; the sailor, coral and shells; the painter, his picture; the girl, a hankerchief of her own sewing. This is right and pleasing, for it restores society in so far to its primary basis, when a man's biography is conveyed in his gift. . . .[68]

In the medieval legend, the juggler brought his performance; and the small child brings her laughter. The thing given, then, is not simply a detachable item, an independent thing in its own right; nor is it to be understood as an external substitute for the giver. It is a *token* of him, that is, it is not only *his*: it is *he*.

This underscores the risk already mentioned, for if the intended recipient rejects the gift, the giver himself is thereby rejected. The extended hand is a gesture of openness, but it can be brushed aside. In extending a gift, the giver exposes himself, thereby opening up his own being to rejection. If the gift is refused, his openness is betrayed. We have already seen that the recipient

is also vulnerable. So, too, our physical posture il-
lustrates this vulnerability and embodies it, for the
open arms of a welcoming embrace expose us and
stand at the opposite to the closed fist and defensive
crouch of someone on his guard. To receive may be
to admit more than what is needed and to acquire
more than what is possessed. For the receiver the
reception is critical because, in receiving the donor
himself, he may receive more than he wants. The
endowment from which the interiority of the bond
issues may be good, ambivalent or worse, so that a
gift may be flawed, not only by a refusal or malac-
ceptance on the part of the recipient, but by the intention of the endowment on the part of the donor
as well. Once again, it is of such contamination that
Peguy speaks when he asks the poor to forgive *us*
the bread we give them. It is not uncommon to feel
an obligation attaching to the reception of a gift,
and this may be freely taken up in gratitude.
Marcel has pointed out that, to the extent to which
life is accepted as a gift, it is a call for a pledge of
fidelity. The existentialist anti-hero of recent
romantic and philosophical literature, on the contrary, protests against the burden of a life which he
must bear without having been consulted beforehand. Of course, we often welcome a gift from a
tangle of motives, not always without greed, but
often with joy at the symbolic presence of the giver
who in the gift is brought into a new association
with us. Such joy does not, of course, refute the vulnerability or remove the risk; it simply confirms the
crisis by its glad surprise.

Suppose now that we modify the simple gift situation by introducing into it a complicating factor. We have already pointed out the inveterate non-parity between donor and recipient; but let us introduce an additional inequality between giver and receiver. Let the receiver be the original donor who makes it possible for the giver to give a gift. The situation becomes that of donor, giver, gift and receiver who is the original donor:

$$d: (g - sg - r = d).$$

An everyday family example will illustrate the modified situation. The parents of a small child provide it with the very means by which it can give them some little gift. Now, in giving the gift the child actualizes the possibility which its parents have provided. Of course, the child subsumes their endowment and fashions its own characteristic response which can be made only by it, and so it has further determined the possibility through its own initiative and character.[69]

What are we to make of this? Is such a "giving" genuine? It would be quite mistaken, I think, to look upon it as empty sham and mere childish play-acting on the grounds that nothing is actually given to the parents which they did not already have or could easily have; or to see its only value in the formation of habits of generosity for later life. Quite to the contrary, the very "nullity" of the little gift as a value in and of itself renders it transparent, so that perceptive parents can see the true value of the gift to lie in the child's expression of affection. The child gives nothing of value — except itself. The gift is the symbolic delivery of itself into the receiving hands of its parents, the "return" of its life to them. Of course, the child may well expect their continuing favour and support, and its motives may be unclear; but in that it is not so unlike an adult. Ontologically, then, the situation reveals these three characteristics: (1) There is inequality in the ontological status and power of the child and its parents; for the parents play a double role, that of setting up the conditions for the child being able to give and that of receiving the gift from it. (2) In many situations the subsistence or independent value of the gift renders it opaque. In this situation the relative "nullity" of the thing given renders the gift transparent, since it has no independent value for the parents. (3) It symbolizes the giver, therefore, making the child present with its love.

We have been considering a relative inequality so far. Although the parents are the principal causes of the life of the child, they are not its only causes, for the child draws continuing life from other persons and things about it. That is why the child can bring to the parents something they have not given to it, — flowers from the field, a water-colour of its own making, or even a smile that reveals its growing personality. But suppose now that we imagine a situation in which there is absolute unconditioned inequality. Here the donor would be the founder of the entire order within which the giver gives and within which the recipient receives. And suppose further that, as in the previous situation, the recipient were the same original donor. Thus,

$$D: [(g - sg - r = D)].$$

The donor institutes the whole order which includes the giver who gives something to the recipient who is the original donor. The donor creates the context within which the giver can give back to the donor something already received from the donor. Now, in this situation nothing can be introduced from outside as from an independent source; the situation is creation *ex nihilo*. To put it in terms of the Biblical religions, the Lord is the donor who institutes the order within which the thing has its value, within which the giver gives, and within which the recipient receives. "O God, you give that I may give."

III

What are we to make of this new situation of absolute inequality? It is a situation of which atheistic humanism has made a great deal. If it is understood in terms of the Biblical religions, the traditional believer will undoubtedly concede that God must withhold his full power from creatures lest they perish. "Man cannot see me and live," says the Lord (*Ex.* 33:19-24); and Jesus says to his disciples: "No one has seen the Father, except he who comes from God." (*John* 6:46) Indeed, the taboos which function in many religions make a similar point. But the withholding of creative power is itself part of the situation, and so the difficulty remains: In such a structure it seems that the sacred gives what is sacred to the sacred. And if that is the situation, can a human being make any real contribution of his own in such a situation? Can there be any integrity to giving and receiving in such a world? Can religious sacrifice, prayer, offering or the service of God have any significance other than the circle of divinity closing upon itself? And is this what is meant when the Bible says that God created the world in order to manifest his glory? What is human, finite and relative seems overwhelmed by what is sacred, infinite and absolute. The air is as close as an incensed altar.

As the atheism of the Enlightenment, based upon the alleged self-sufficiency of natural science and mechanism, deepened into the radical atheism of the nineteenth century, based upon the primacy of man, the will to reject such a religious structure expressed itself in a positive demand for unbelief as the condition of human well-being (Comte, Marx, Nietzsche). It was urged, on general grounds and on the basis of criteria external to the religious structure, that religion is really man's concession to his own impotency and that it is merely a fearful and ineffectual hope for security, an illusion in need of therapy, perhaps also a social and political strategy of priestcraft. Within the structure human action would have to be empty, it was alleged, a sham in which a divine self-identity would absorb everything else. (And, indeed, is not the speech of the prophet a heteronomous speech? Does he not utter someone else's word, a strange speech in which what passes between human speaker and human listener is owned by neither? And does not St. Paul boast that he does nothing and that God alone works in him?) Genuine action, including that of giving, seems to require genuine diversity of being, power and will, whereas the structure set out above seems to deny to man his own freedom since it denies to him everything that might be his own work. But even if the structure were not empty, it would be intolerable on its own terms, for even a child can surprise its parents by bringing them something not received from them and which lies outside their power. But within this structure, giving would be both necessary and humiliating. It would be necessary, because the situation of absolute inequality would have to be acknowledged (*obligatio, religio*); and it would be humiliating, because it would be futile as well as compulsory. The condition of absolute inequality and the divine circularity seem to make any attempt of man to reciprocate to God a vain and empty gesture. Indeed, according to the Christian doctrine of grace the very reception of the original gift is itself first received from God. And indeed, if creation *ex nihilo* is taken in its radical sense, then not only the endowment but the reception must also be part of the original gift. The case against such a religious situation comes down to this: the radical inequality suffocates man and his possibilities, and the divine circularity empties his giving and all his activity of reality. In denying him creativity, religion becomes man's opium. Unbelief offers itself as the only defence of human autonomy. Indeed, Sartre's characters writhe under the shame of having to receive even from other humans; and Mauriac's *Woman of the Pharisees* uses her "gifts" to bind everyone to her. How much more would the "gifts" of an absolutely transcendent God bind!

At this point the conception of an absolutely all-powerful God, creator *ex nihlo*, seems utterly outmoded. Surely progressive man has grown beyond such a primitive notion as he comes of age. Is it not a kindness to put away such an oppressive obstacle to the dignity and freedom that man has already won in any event? It seems only decent, then, to proclaim the death of God. Or, if he is not dead, then at least that he is finite or in process and therefore in mutual interaction with creatures, giving but also receiving from them (W. James, some Whiteheadians). Now what is troublesome about such a situation of absolute inequality is not only his transcendence, but his absoluteness as well. That is why a Hegelian self-developing absolute is not of much help in meeting the atheistic objections. After all, did not Kierkegaard warn us about the danger to the solvency of the individual in an absolute system of the Hegelian sort?

Of course, traditional Biblical religion can frame an explanation of its rejection by atheism.

(1) Its most immediate interpretation and evalua-
tion of the atheistic refusal to accept the religious
situation is to understand it as *sin,* man's turning
away from the very conditions of his salvation. (2)
Since the refusal is viewed as a failure of knowledge, a darkening of the light, the sin is *unbelief.*
And (3) since it is a breaking of a relationship already given, it is *infidelity.* On the other hand, in
traditional Christianity, the *possibility* of refusal is
seen as the condition for the freedom of accepting
the relationship.

Unbelief sees it differently. We began with a
simple situation of giving and receiving and seem
to have been caught up into a perverse form of
domination. We have extended the category of
the gift to a situation of absolute inequality between donor and recipient, and we have done this
in order to understand better the meaning of creation *ex nihilo*; but our strategy seems to have failed, or to have succeeded too well. If man is to
communicate with a creator *ex nihilo*, must he not
pay the price of absorption into the circle of the
divine creative power? Is not such a God the natural predator of man? Some Christians may
throw up their hands and cry out: "But you don't
understand the situation! It is not a power-
relation at all; it is a love-relation. Our God is a
God of Love." But the shift from power to love
does not seem, on the face of it as least, to over-
come the difficulty. An overwhelming love may be
a gentle yoke, yet where in its soft coils is man?
To many of our contemporaries there seems no

escape but to refuse to respond. *Non serviam*: I will not give my consent. If God initiates the context and sets the conditions for performance, then man is pressed to play a role that is already determined and not his own. And this evacuation of man seems brought to its extreme by a creation which determines everything about man and the world, even their very possibility. Is it any wonder, then, that Sartre argues more or less as follows: If there were a God worthy of the name, he would have to be all-powerful and free; but then I would not be free; since I will to be free, there is no God?[70] Or that Nietzsche writes: If there were gods, how could I endure not to be one; hence there are no gods?[71] And a Catholic interpreter even adds, somewhat dramatically perhaps, that Nietzsche here gives expression to a desire for the death of God, a desire rooted in the very condition of being a creature.[72]

The difficulty is neither new nor contrived. Even some Christians find the traditional belief in the absolute transcendent power of God to be an unfortunate bar to the full realization of human freedom and responsibility, dignity and creativity. They also find it to be an impediment to any effective *apologia* for a contemporary faith. Finally, they find it difficult, if not impossible, to reconcile the appalling evil in the world with the embarrassing claim to God's absolute transcendent power over it. It seems that the "Good News" can survive only if it disengages itself from transcendence, and *a fortiori* from the most extravagant expression of transcendence, creation *ex nihilo*. In that survival, however, it is not clear just what survives, since such an immanentized faith will have lost its traditional focus.

It is noteworthy that St. Thomas selected only two counterpositions to set against his five ways to the existence of God.[73] They are: (1) Theoretically, an appeal to God is not needed in order to explain things, since recourse to the principles of nature, on the one hand, and to the freedom of man, on the other, suffices. And (2) practically, if there were an all-powerful God, he could not have tolerated so much evil in his creation, unless he were himself a monster. The subsequent career of atheism has played out both of these objections. The scientific atheism of the Enlightenment professed disbelief on putative cognitive grounds: God was neither knowable nor needed to explain man and the world. To this Voltaire added his scorn for the reputed benevolence of God. The humanistic atheism of Nietzsche and Sartre professed disbelief the better to defend human freedom, dignity and responsibility. Following Feuerbach, Marx raised human *praxis* to the first principle of social reconstruction and explanation ("man alone"). So that these later humanistic atheisms are those of will and action.[74] They are practical more than theoretical in origin and intent. Nevertheless, the decision of the atheistic humanist to eradicate belief in God is based upon his understanding of the situation in which an allegedly all-powerful God stands over against and above man and his world.

It seems appropriate, then, to attempt to provide a cognitive solution of the issues raised by the atheist's understanding of creation *ex nihilo*. These issues arise in the face of the radical inequality that is inseparable from absolute giving and receiving. The contemporary atheist puts them in the form of two objections: (1) A creator *ex nihilo* would make impossible the ontological otherness of man, his self-subsistence and independence; and (2) it would make impossible man's freedom, his effective agency, autonomy and creativity. In a word, in such a situation man would be robbed of his genuine possibilities and his responsibility.

The atheistic humanist alleges that man would suffer a radical humiliation in such a situation. Now humiliation or indignity is a state of degradation. In its ordinary meaning degradation implies a process from a prior, more worthy state; and in its ordinary meaning a state presupposes a subject. Such a state is posterior to and dependent upon its subject; so that the subject itself bears the capacity for a different and better state. The atheistic humanist, however, raises humiliation to transcendental import. He alleges that if there were a creator *ex nihilo*, then the human condition would be one of abject and total dependence; so that the only worthy response on man's part would be to abolish the very structure itself through the free production of meaning out of himself. (Hence, Marx's "man alone," and the secular atheisms of Nietzsche and Sartre.) Moreover, the atheist refuses to avoid the problem by relativizing the creator, as though it could become a more or less equal party in interaction with man. In any event such a relativism abandons the issues by abandonning the conception of a creator *ex nihilo*. The atheist, on the other hand, does not ignore the conception; he seeks to deny its validity. He doesn't want compromise; he wants refutation.

To attribute humiliation to someone is to measure his present condition by reference to some other condition in which he might have been or could yet be. When the atheist says, therefore, that man is humiliated if he is a creature, he measures his being a creature in comparison with another possiblity, viz., that of not being a creature. That is, the atheist interprets the putative humiliation of being-a-creature in terms of a putative integrity that man would have (really can have?) outside that structure. Now this is not to find a defect within the creational structure taken in its own terms. It is to state his own conviction in favour of one structure (non-creational) against another (creational); but it is not to put forth an objection against creation. Instead of making an objection against creation on its own grounds he covertly asserts his own position, viz., that man has an intrinsic dignity only insofar as he is not created. This surreptitious (and perhaps unwitting) transference from one structure to the other is the source of the allegation that creation *ex nihilo* contradicts itself when it affirms both the integrity of the creature and its absolute dependence. This is certainly an important and legitimate issue:

How can a creature be absolutely dependent in its being and also have ontological integrity? Is this a contradiction or is it not? That is a fair question.

The atheistic humanist, for his part, holds that the double assertion is contradictory. But he attempts to show this by absolutizing some form of what Marcel called "the techniques of human degradation."[75] Now, any attempt to absolutize them does, indeed, end in contradiction. Suppose that the creator is an absolute tyrant. Then, if the one suffering humiliation (the creature) is in fact a mere shadow, a plaything, simply a puppet without integrity, the humiliation rebounds upon the torturer and verges on self-mutilation. Sadism turns into masochism, and the creator-tyrant is discredited. If, on the other hand, the one suffering humiliation has even a minimal subsistence, if he is even a slight self, then a cry of indignant protest against the torturer rises in our throats: You have no right to the absolute disposal of the sufferer! And once again the creator-tyrant is discredited. Up with the banner of atheistic humanism, down with the dehumanizing belief in a creator *ex nihilo*! It is true that the attempt to absolutize humiliation bears the contradiction by which the creator-tyrant needs the otherness of the sufferer (the creature) in order simultaneously and in the same process both to obliterate the other (rendering it worthless) and yet to sustain the other (in order to visit the degradation upon it). Long before Sartre and atheistic humanism, Hegel had parlayed the drama of this conflict into the provi-

sional stalemate of the "unhappy consciousness,"[76] and had pointed out the contradiction inherent in this state of mind. Moreover, the one-
sided nature of the resolution proposed by atheistic humanism is manifest in its anthropocentric
weight and the arbitrary restrictions it places
upon the central conceptions of freedom and
power. Then, too, the purported "objections"
against creation *ex nihilo* are really assertions of a
point of view, which imports into the creational
structure the very conceptions of autonomy and
heteronomy, of power and dependence, that are
guaranteed to undermine it.

To determine whether in truth there are genuine objections to creation *ex nihilo* that show it to
be wrong or inadequate in important ways, the
meaning of creaturely integrity and creative
power need to be examined afresh within the context of creation *ex nihilo* itself. Only then can we
relate it to the whole of our experience and
thought.

It is necessary, first of all, to continue the consideration of the challenge of atheistic humanism,
since if it were to carry the day in terms of the
creational structure itself, as it claims to do, then
creation *ex nihilo* would be condemned out of its
own mouth. And so we ask, within the creational
structure itself, whether the absolute dependence
of the creature is or could be a condition of essential and radical indignity and humiliation. Now,
within the creational context, the creatureliness of
the creature, — its being-a-creature, — is not a re-

ceived condition which it *has*; nor, strictly speaking, is being-a-creature even a received condition that it *is*; rather, the received condition itself is *it*. The dependence of the creature is absolute because it is dependence upon that very generosity that in its turn is the original condition of the creature's very being. If the creature were humiliated by this, then its very being would be in a totally deprived and absolutely abject state; so that the creature would be *nihil*, rather than *ex nihilo*. Now, in touching upon St. Anselm's discussion, I suggested that creation is the original gift, a giving out of absolute privation. It follows that the creatureliness of the creature (the received condition) is not a nullity, but is rather the ingress of the creature into being; so that, on the basis of that ingress, can be seen the absolute *nihil* that was the creature's meontological predecessor. The creature is *ex nihilo*, that is, it stands *outside of* absolute privation by virtue of the creative generosity. This creative generosity is the ground for the absolute inequality between creator and creature, that very inequality that has raised the threat to the creature's integrity. But that same creative generosity is also the ground for the very being of the creature.

Moreover, since the creative generosity does not extend simply to individuals singly, but in creating them creates their world as well, the creature is in fact a member *of* the ultimate plurality, the created universe.[77] More than that, it is by its very nature and being a member *for* this plurality.

It participates in the plurality, and the plurality in and through it. Now, no member of a plurality can be humiliated by the primary condition that makes possible (1) the plurality essential to the member, (2) its membership in the plurality, and (3) its own being as well. That is, not unless humiliation were the first and the last word, and every word between, engulfing the plurality and its members. Nor is it possible to isolate man, this "thinking reed," and arrogate to him the foundations of truth and value, in the manner recommended by atheistic humanism. For his interdependence with non-human as well as human beings is so patent and so indispensable for his own being, worth and thought that it would be nothing short of impossible for him to produce the intelligible and the valuable out of radically anti-intelligible and valueless absurdity. In the context of creation, there can be no plurality, no relation of membership and no members to be humiliated without the original founding endowment. Humiliation and indignity are relative to that original presupposition. They are specific evils that rest upon a transcendental generosity. They are founded upon, derivative from and ontologically posterior to the foundational ingress into being. In creation, the original endowment makes the plurality and its individuals both possible and actual; and *that* endowment itself cannot be identified with humiliation, since it is the presupposition of any such secondary condition. In a word, there must be something in order that something

might be humiliated. The endowment is the presupposition of any such possibility. Subsequent
factors would have to be introduced to account for
humiliation.

Of course, it might be suggested that the
original creative endowment is just for the sake of
having a creature to humiliate. Indeed, this has
been suggested by the dark meditation upon divinity in Brownings's *Caliban upon Setebos*:

> Let twenty pass, and stone the twenty-first.
> Loving not, hating not, just choosing so.

An absurd world for the victims, to be sure! I will
argue shortly, however, that cruel tyranny could
not sustain the creature in its integrity; and the
full intent of creation *ex nihilo* is to maintain the integrity of the creature as well as its absolute dependence. Both atheistic humanism and tyranni-
cal theism travel along the same circle: either God
or man, but not both.

We have been discussing the ontological features of a dynamic plurality because the total
effect of the creative activity is not a loose collection of individuals; it is a world of created beings.
The created world is the totality of all totalities,
the most extensive dynamic plurality of beings
and their factors. Within it there is movement, interaction, communication, and, in the broadest
and deepest sense, giving and receiving. For these
are endemic to any dynamic plurality, and without them it can neither be established nor maintained. Within the world we can distinguish dif-

ferent kinds of plurality: for example, the natural, the organic and the social forms of organization. Each has its proper mode of communication, and can be examined according to its terms. But it is also possible to examine the world as a whole in terms of the mode of communication appropriate to one of its forms of organization: for example, the physical and chemical transference of energy characteristic of the world of inanimate nature is operative in the inner-directed transformation of the environment carried out by organisms, and also in the behavioural interaction between members of animal or human society. Within the limits of such an analysis a certain equivalence of impetus and resistance is observable in the exchange of physical and chemical energy. Then, too, organic life is maintained by a balance of inner and outer forces. And mutual exchange is even essential to human society (*commercium*). In terms of physics and mechanics, a billiard ball's impetus is met by the resistance of the ball it strikes; in terms of physiology, there is stimulus and response; and in sociology, there are the dynamics of social interaction. Within the limits of such an analysis we can report a sort of equivalence in kind and degree between the impulse and the reception at impact. This is what we mean when we say that, in a closed classical system, an action is countered by an equal and opposite reaction; or when we say that *ideally* stimulus should equal response.

Yet, as I have already remarked, there is non-reciprocity as well in each of these forms of organization and communication, that is, in the natural, organic and social. It is possible to regard the second law of thermodynamics as a minimal expression of a certain irreversibility and non-reciprocity in the flow of energy, whereby the free energy available for further transformation decreases with each transformation (entropy), though this law rests upon certain presuppositions about the nature of the physical universe. The ontological difference between giver and receiver, the "distance" opened up by the non-reciprocity that is inseparable from giving and receiving, increases with the increasing complexity of the plurality and its members. Moreover, the non-reciprocity is not one of entropy or decline in possibilities. When parent organisms give life to their young, whatever satisfaction may come to the parents by reciprocation from the young (in the case of the higher animals, for instance, which rear them), it is different in kind, weight and degree from the gift the young receive from their parents. The non-reciprocity is greater, because it is a difference of another order: life itself is given, whereas some satisfaction is received in turn. And so, too, the health restored to me by the physician is not matched by the fee I pay him. The distance can be acknowledged (and this, indeed, is part of the appropriate reception), but it cannot be traversed. The receiver is indelibly marked by having received what cannot be returned. It is true of all such values: power, life, health, freedom and knowl-

we are indebted to the endowment we have received from others edge. None of these fundamental values can be reciprocated, although they can be handed on. Such non-reciprocity is built into the dynamic plurality of existence and life at its deepest and broadest level. It is the indispensable transcendental generosity needed for the establishment and maintenance of a dynamic plurality, the profligacy that is inseparable from it.

Now the world which results from creation is not a mere loose collection of units which happen to produce the plurality as a resultant sum. Rather, the plurality is the units *and* their being together.[78] Indeed, their being units at all includes their being units *of* a plurality. Now this mutuality of the units is the indispensable condition for their being members of the plurality, and since their very nature (*ratio*) is such that they could not be without being members, this mutuality is the indispensable ground of their being as units. Since it is not possible to disengage their membership from their simply being (except by an abstract analysis which deliberately leaves out their membership, and thereby distorts their nature), it follows that the radical generosity required by the dynamic plurality is the original condition for the basic, shared values that are constitutive of the plurality itself and of the units as well. In any communication within the plurality, there is a specific character that is realized insofar as things are themselves units, or groups of units, and there is a transcendental character ingredient in the same communication insofar as things are

members of the plurality and participants in its
inherent liberality. That is why we have been able
to discern in a gift, in addition to its specific
values, transcendental values which it embodies
and communicates, and which are fundamental
conditions for the plurality, the membership and
the units. These transcendental values include existence, power and life, but also individuality, relation and otherness. Moreover, these values are
not merely minimal conditions for the units or
merely external to them. On the contrary, they
play an intrinsic role in enriching the unit's membership in the plurality. None of these ultimate
values, nor for that matter their corresponding
disvalues, — neither good nor evil, — is something
to be transferred from one unit to another as a
detachable object. They are values or disvalues,
because they are not indifferent conditions; they
do not leave the plurality and its units untouched.
They are the goods or evils on which the very survival or annihilation of the plurality itself depends, and the very well-being or devaluation of
its units.

The condition for a dynamic plurality of beings
to exist is that they receive from others. Since man
is a member of the ultimate dynamic plurality,
giving and receiving are so pervasive and radical
that they constitute the very condition for being
human. To protest against the reception, saying
that it is a humiliation, is to protest against the
very conditions that make human being and human dignity possible; and to protest against the

very conditions that make the protest possible.
But this is to embrace contradiction and absurdity. Giving and receiving are the radical conditions
without which man could not be. They are the
foundation of his being, his own ontological good.
All other goods are subsequent to that. The original endowment of which creation *ex nihilo* speaks
is the first and indispensable ontological good
without which other values and disvalues could
not count because they would not be at all. All
further considerations are founded upon that original good. In the human order, the specific objects which men hand one another are symbols of
a deeper giving and receiving, for they are signs
that embody the generosity of their shared being
as members of a dynamic plurality. The gift,
then, is the medium in and through which giver
and recipient affirm their being-in-the-world-
together. It is the place of the celebration of their
co-presence.

We need to see, however, not only *that* giving
and receiving are indispensable and integral to
being human, but also *how* it is possible to receive
everything and yet to maintain an intrinsic dignity and integrity. If the creator's giving and receiving presupposes an absolute inequality, *how* can
man receive with dignity and respond with integrity? We must take our cue from human experience itself. Human beings are involved in a variety
of relationships, but there is one mode of relation
that is constitutive of consciousness itself, and it
promises the possibility of association between

unequals that is compatible with the integrity of
both parties to the relation. Adapting Aristotle's
saying about the soul, St. Thomas frequently
remarks that it can in a manner become all
things.[79] This capacity also led Hegel to find the
distinctive character of spirit (*Geist*) in something
like consciousness, saying that only consciousness
could tolerate the contradiction of the other,
recognize its otherness, pass over into it, and yet
retain and recover itself in the process.[80] More
recently, phenomenologists, existentialists and
others have emphasized the intentional character
of consciousness (*conscience de. . .*), in that consciousness is attentive to the other as it is in its
otherness.

Objectification has frequently been criticized
insofar as it has been understood to be an attitude
of the mind whereby it posits its objects as abstract products of its hidden methodological presuppositions, or as something alien standing over
against its own subjectivity. But the spirit of
objectivity in its best sense is the inherent and distinctive thrust of consciousness towards realizing
its own capacity through opening itself out on to
the world of beings.[81] Now, such an objectivity
requires that consciousness be intentionally present to another in terms of the other's own being.
Thus, for example, a scholar only comes to know
a subject if he lives with it, gets inside of it, so to
speak, becomes intimate with its fuller meaning,
as the entymologist Fabre lived with his beloved
insects. In the relationship, the enquirer's curiosi-

ty, his methods and criteria as well as the face which the thing turns toward him, — all of this sets the slant of his knowledge. Still, to the degree that he is to succeed in knowing his subject at all, to that extent he must bring a readiness to submit to the appropriate demands of the other. It is as though the subject-matter were to say to him: "This is what you must do, if you would really come to know me." Caught up by the theoretical power of his presuppositions the enquirer may be tempted to shut up the evidence before it is finished speaking to him; indeed, it never finishes. Listen to Fabre as he calls to his insects:

> Come here, one and all of you — you, the sting-bearers, and you, the wing-cased armour-clads — take up my defence and bear witness in my favour. Tell of the intimate terms on which I live with you, of the patience with which I observe you, of the care with which I record your actions. Your evidence is unanimous:. . .and whoso cares to question you in his turn will obtain the same replies.[82]

It is a homely example; but, no matter how complex and interwoven with subjectivity and with theoretical preoccupations the enquiry may be, its subject-matter places an unconditional demand upon the enquirer that he respect its integrity, even as he enters into relationship with it. Indeed, if the subject-matter of the enquiry does not retain its integrity or if the enquirer does not respect it, he will inevitably distort it and fail to know it, for he will fail in that degree to be present with it just as it is. For although knowledge must have its subjective moment (self-consciousness), it must also have its objective moment. Now this latter is the requirement that the knower be with the known on the terms of the known. The knower must submit to the discipline of the thing to be known.

There is an aspect of discipline in love, too, and especially in that love that is the capacity to associate with another in a way that respects the integrity of the other. There is a kind of love that is a presence to another in which the lover is concerned to wish the other well: *amor benevolentiae.* It has three aspects: the risk of generosity, the satisfaction of subjectivity and the discipline of objectivity. Benevolence obviously contains an ingredient of generosity within it, and the ungenerous are incapable of extending it to others. Generosity is that spirit of abandon with which the lover breaks beyond the limits of autonomy and heteronomy, beyond the seemingly safe territory where mine is mine and yours is yours, into an intentional relation wherein the good of the beloved is in the lover's concern without being in his possession. It is as though the lover has adopted a second centre, as though he has redistributed his concern, so that the good of the beloved has equal weight (*pondus*) with his own.

But there is an aspect of subjective satisfaction, too. The ingredient of subjectivity appropriate to benevolent love is the satisfaction enjoyed by the lover in his association with the beloved as he gives himself over to the spell of the beloved. It is obvious that the element of subjective satisfaction needs to be restrained, lest it overwhelm the beloved and corrupt the relationship. But neither should the element of satisfaction be wholly suppressed, as is suggested by some of the talk about "being a person for others." It is misleading to obscure the ingredient of self that is essential to any healthy love. For without self-worth, the lover has nothing to offer the beloved, and without self-satisfaction the lover can take no joy in the goodness of the beloved. If the lover recognizes the element of self in his love, he is the less likely to let it intrude surreptitiously into the relationship to the injury of both parties. Benevolence, therefore, is neither egoism nor altruism. For it is not only a shift of weight or expansion to a second centre, it is also the qualitative transformation of the very nature of self-satisfaction. In benevolence the lover takes his own joy in what is good for the other; he enjoys the good that the beloved enjoys; he takes satisfaction in what is genuinely satisfactory for the other.

Now, it is just here that the discipline of objectivity shows itself in benevolent love. For genuine love is the giving of oneself with respect for the other. It is not an indiscriminate giving without consideration for the capacity and freedom of the recipient. False love is giving with an abandon that is still centered in a hidden way upon a self that has not yet attained an objective respect for the integrity of the other. Genuine love may not reckon the cost to the giver, but it does reckon the cost to the recipient. When such love is properly

received, it can be a strength that helps to bring
about the genuine possibilities of the beloved,
even possibilities that would not exist without the
love. False love, on the other hand, realizes the
possibilities of the lover by betraying the integrity
of the beloved. Genuine love is desire under the
inner constraint of the beloved; it is subjective
passion disciplining itself creatively in and
through the presence of the beloved. In a word,
then, there are relationships in which there can be
the giving of oneself to another while respecting
the integrity of the other. Through them, it is
possible to give without usurpation and to receive
without humiliation. The tension and the risk that
attend all giving and receiving are still there, for
without them there would be no generosity. But
the willing discipline of objectivity is there too;
and, when all goes well, the transformed satisfaction of subjectivity is present in benevolent love as
well. These three are constitutive of this distinctive and highly determinate relationship; so that,
through understanding and love, we have access
to the transcendental as well as to the specific
energies operative in giving and receiving, — and
even to an obscure hint of love that exceeds any
we are capable of.

The preceding analysis is meant to have shown
that an absolute giving is compatible with the integrity and dignity of the creature and with the
freedom of human receptivity. It has sought to
clarify the conception of creation *ex nihilo*. If we
were to put that conception into play, we would

have to show that there is actual creation, and this would require us to mount a proof that would show that the transcendental aspects of giving and receiving can be grounded only in an original giving whose source can only be the actually existing creator, this "most liberal giver." Such a proof lies beyond the intent of the present lecture, which is attempting to analyze and clarify the meaning of gift as the mode appropriate to creative causality. In furthering that clarification we need to outline the way the three aspects of benevolent love function in creative causality: creative generosity, creative subjectivity and creative objectivity.

Generosity is inseparable from all giving. It is the primal reality at the source of the breaking forth accomplished in giving; for giving is a deed: it is done, something is given. Generosity nourishes the reality of power that is fused with the intentionality of intelligence to form the communication. In terms of creative causality, generosity expresses itself as the power that brings creatures and their world *ex nihilo* into being. Now, such a creating power is not an extravagant display of physical or trans-physical force, a sort of cosmic super-power, a celestial megaton bomb in reverse. Creative activity is not to be understood in terms of the lowest common denominator among the modes of power.

Nor is it to be understood in terms of an indeterminate concept of causality. Such a general concept of causality is simply not definitive enough to sustain the unique and unexampled de-

terminacy of creative causation. This may not
have been so obvious as long as the medieval notion of causality was rich enough to carry implicit-
ly the sense of the higher modes of causality; as
long, for example, as it was generally accepted
that intelligence and being are convertible (*ens et
verum convertuntur*), that the exercize of power was
at root the activity of intelligence, and that cosmic
power was associated with order and wisdom.
With the subsequent modern reduction of causal
power to that exercized in physical nature alone,
however, the general concept of causative power
has become increasingly empty and unable to
support the requirements of creation *ex nihilo*.

In this present essay, the turn to the category of
giving is not meant to place an anthropological or
"merely subjective" restriction upon causative
power; quite to the contrary, it intends the opening out of the category of causality to richer and
more definitive forms and potencies. And we are
justified in taking this turn on the general grounds
that what holds really and truly at the level of
human life is as apt for analysis of the ultimate
nature of reality as is the methodologically restricted concept of power-as-physical-force operative in the objective consideration of physical
nature. The objectification of nature (and by extension, of the human as well) is promoted today
with impressive results. It proceeds in the name of
external criteria of verification and in accord with
the acceptance of the world as a set of given facts
(*data*) to give its account of reality in terms of ex-

ternal relations. Such objective study will and
must go on. It is a precious contribution to our
understanding, and in the form of scientific technology it alone can provide the means for meeting
many of the problems of contemporary existence.
But we have seen that it takes the world as a start-
ing point from which to construct experiments,
hypotheses and techniques that seek to control the
repetible dimensions of things. Its external grasp
of evidence does not carry us into the region of ul-
timacy, so that ultimate questions are then left to
religious faith (bereft of the support of rational
understanding), or — what is at least as likely — to
the misapplication of a scientific theory to an in-
appropriate field, or — what is worse — to vague
opinions confirmed by shifting opinion polls. The
withdrawal over recent centuries of much of philosophical and scientific intelligence from the interiority of nature is not simply a particular
change in philosophical theory; it is the retreat of
discourse from an entire intellectual domain. It is
not uncommon today to counteract the withdrawal of interiority from nature (objectification)
by a process of subjectification that heightens
man's own interiority. This is the modern anthropological turn characteristic of recent centuries in
European and American culture.[83]

The interpretation of creative causality through
the category of gift, on the other hand, restores a
metaphysical interiority to nature, as well as to
the natural in man. By metaphysical interiority I
mean that which accounts for the intelligibility

without which nature could not enter into scientific and philosophical enquiry; that which accounts
for the serviceability by which it can play its role
in human technology, meshing with human purpose; that which accounts for its availability to
religion in its sacraments and symbols, and in
other ways, to literature, art and music; indeed,
to what Hegel called the works of spirit. But, first
of all, by the metaphysical interiority of nature I
mean its own immediate inner ground of integrity, the proper foundation upon which it rests its
own "right" to claim respect. Now, this metaphysical interiority cannot be confirmed or even
reached by external methods of objectification. It
is a rich metaphysical texture grouded in the intimate presence of the creative cause to the things
of nature, and to the natural in man. In and
through the category of gift we can recover the
metaphysical interiority of nature, since the analysis permits us to see the outlines of a causality
that is fully determinate, both as to its mode: it is
intelligent, voluntary and loving, and as to what
is communicated: the most determinate and decisive actuality, the very existence of the world
and its creatures.

Now, this highly determinate causality is characterized by the identification of power with love.
Often enough we encounter power in indifferent,
uncaring or even hostile form. This is the dark
mystery of contending forces that threatens even
the conception of benevolent love when it is
understood as absolute creative power. It is the

scandal—not of the mere possibility of evil—but of its actual existence. Within the limits of this lecture, and mindful of the lectures given on this topic already in this series, it is only possible to remember that—far from being able to "solve" the "problem" of evil—all of one's intellectual acuity and spiritual courage is required simply to contain it, even in the order of analysis. But by a paradox that is the ground for hope, it should be recognized that there could be no evil in a universe created by an absolutely benevolent love, *if* its creatures did not possess their own integrity, and were not bent upon realizing their own possibilities, including for some of them their free possibilities. But so they were made. Indeed, if creatures as we know them lacked their own integrity, it is difficult to see how they could be the product of an absolutely benevolent love. Here we are at the centre of the ontological tension between creator and creature, a tension that the benevolent love could have avoided by not creating at all, but which it sustains rather than removes. What great good is to be realized by this universe, that a benevolent love should create it in the face of the possibility—might we even say, the likelihood—of great evil?

It is against this sombre backdrop, then, that we must place the identification of creative power with radical love. There can be no such essential identification of human power with human love. Both remain in some way abstract; this is the tension peculiar to the creature, and of which man is

especially aware. To be sure, the human lover
does not make an empty gesture of good will when
he "gives spiritual support" to his beloved. He
rallies his resources and powers, and expends the
totality of his energies to sustain the beloved if
need be. Nevertheless, a human lover finds his actual power tragically limited, so that he feels an
uneasy gap between what he wills for the beloved
and what he can actually do for the beloved. This
is because human love is the fusion of actual
energies with an intention that may remain unfulfilled. The non-coincidence of intent and actuality
can be a source of anguish for the human lover.
The absolute creative power, on the other hand,
can *voluntarily* withhold itself for the good of the
creature and its integrity or freedom. But, just
because it is absolute, there can be no *necessary*
distance between intention and fulfillment, no
restriction upon creative power, no emptiness in
creative intent: power and intent are one and the
same. In creation, a "most liberal giving" institutes or establishes *ex nihilo* creatures and their
world. It thereby also constitutes and sustains
them. This absolute fusion of power and love, of
reality and intent, of effective determination and
total concern brings about the existence of creatures whose integrity even the creator freely respects in keeping with the very character of his
benevolence.

Does risk remain for such an absolute giver?
The answer must be: yes; for at the centre of creative giving lurks the dark possibility of evil. Just

because the creator is a lover and just because creation is the generosity of a thoroughly radical love,
just because that love respects the integrity and dignity of the creature, and just because that love wills
into existence a beloved who can respond in freedom — and therefore, badly or well, — how could
such a universe be and yet not carry within it the
possibility of evil? To be sure, a bad reception of the
creator's gift does not inflict upon him a wound to
his being in its subsistence; just as, in many in-
stances, a human lover does not lose something of
his proper being, the being he possessed before he
offered love and was refused. But, as with human
lovers, so too with divine, the creator can receive a
wound to his being *as a lover*. In his creative activity
he makes an offer of being, and in that offering he
exposes himself as a potential victim of malaccept-
ance. Of course, because the creative offer of being
is absolutely radical, it would be quite wrong to imagine that, before the offer is actually made, the
creature waits in some state of possibility in order to
accept or reject the gift. For the recipient of that
radical gift only comes into being with it. No creature is consulted before it is created, because there
is no creature to consult. We are, indeed, at the
beginning. Nor does any creature ask to be created,
or hover in the wings, like an actor worrying about
his lines and waiting to be called on stage. Still, we
are justified in speaking of creation as an offer. For
it is freely given being, a sort of ontological credit
advanced for subsequent realization in and through
the career of the creature.

Moreover, since the "most liberal giver" does not give out of need, but rather for the good of the recipient, the evil that comes through creaturely malfeasance is the evil that infects the creature and not the creator. The creator is "moved" by the fate of the creature because of his *own* concern for the creature. The "movement," to speak improperly, is intransitive; that is, it is not brought about by the transitive action of the creature. Indeed, even with human lovers, the plight of the beloved does not affect the lover in the same way as a productive force effects a product. The relation is intransitive in its essential nature. The intransitivity of the relation of knowing and loving does not mean that the knower and the lover are not attentive to what is known and loved. On the contrary, it is only in and through such intransitivity that there can be knowing loving concern. In creative activity there is a unique intransitivity. For, because he is absolute, the creator knows and loves the creature out of his knowledge and love of himself, and not out of any dependence upon the creature. His concern for the creature rises up in him through his own unconditioned self-knowledge and self-love. It is not that the creator is unconcerned with the fate of the creatures he has made; quite to the contrary, his concern flows from his unconditioned generosity.

We have come again by another route upon the absolute inequality between creatures and their creative donor; and also upon the absolute non-reciprocity between the creative donor and the creaturely recipient. The medieval schoolmen expressed this absolute non-reciprocity by saying that God is related to creatures only by a relation of reason, whereas creatures are related to God by a real relation of causal dependence and participation.[84] To this we can add the modern sense of intentionality, which is a kind of intransitivity, and according to which relations of knowing and loving concern are intentional. The relation of God to creatures is intentional, then, not only in the sense that it is not a real reciprocity after the manner of an interaction in which both parties undergo transmutation; but rather because the relation of God to creatures is like a relation of consciousness. Moreover, it is like a relation of consciousness that, out of its own generosity rather than out of any dependence upon creatures, is fully attuned to them in loving concern. The category of gift helps us to understand such knowing and loving concern, and to understand as well the nature of the risk undertaken by the generosity that characterizes radical creative love.

Because of the absolute, unconditioned and unconditional nature of creative love, it might seem that neither subjective satisfaction nor objective discipline could be associated with it. But in truth we can speak of a divine self-worth that is absolute and of a self-satisfaction that is the unconditional joy of the creator in the good of the beloved, a joy that springs from no need in the creator, but rather out of the admiration and pride of the worker in his workmanship. The Biblical tradi-

tion gives religious expression to this joy: for the
Lord looked at what he had made and saw that it
was good, and so seeing he blessed it. And the
Biblical tradition once again gives religious expression to the manifestation of this joy: it is the
glory of God the creator shining before his creation. In philosophical terms, the moment of self-
satisfaction, — already transformed in human
benevolent love into a joy for the sake of the other,
— now in creative self-satisfaction is utterly transformed into a concern that is identical with the
genuine good of the creature. So that the glory
and the goodness, the subjectivity and the objectivity of creative love is wholly and entirely the integral good of the creature willed by the creator.

It may be well to emphasize once again, however, that the objectivity in creative love is not a
condition imposed upon the creator by the creature, for then the creative love would not be absolute and unconditioned. The objectivity operative
in creative love, then, is not, as with human
lovers, a conditioned objectivity in which the
lover stands in real, although intransitive and
intentional relation to the object loved. Rather,
the objectivity is the creator's, and it holds insofar
as he freely determines to create a creature of a
certain sort with integrity and freely determines to
respect that integrity. In creating creatures who
have freedom, he even determines to respect the
capacity to flaw the original gift. The German
word, *Opfer,* catches both meanings, for the creator's love is both an offering and, potentially, a

victim. Theories of divine creative ideas (St. Augustine) and of exemplar causality (St. Bonaventure) catch the element of self-possessed objectivity in the creator. They must be completed, of course, with the reminder that by its very nature creative activity does not only bring about types of being, or even a world of being, but individual beings themselves. And we need to remember, too, the risk that arises not out of *thought* about creation, but only with the *actual* giving. And with that we come to the drama of creation: the conferring of actual existence *ex nihilo*.

IV

Along with others, I have found St. Thomas especially helpful, because he hands on a light for our journey to the centre of the created world. That light is his understanding of *being (ens)*. He tells us that we can speak of prime matter as created, and of forms and accidents as created too, but only indirectly insofar as they come to be in the production of a being *(productio entis)*. Now, by recognizing in his metaphysics the primacy of being, St. Thomas is simply redeeming the initial promise uttered in our first knowing encounter with things.[85] For in that encounter what first strikes the mind is that things in some way *are,* and so we necessarily attribute the name *being* to everything we apprehend. A Kantian may be expected to object: But is this not the merely apparent necessity by which data must be submitted to

the *a priori* conditions of the human mind? St.
Thomas is surprised, instead, with some ingredient in things themselves that draws the mind forth
into the judgment: *that things are.* Not that they
seem, but that they are. For the primary inclina-
tion of the judgment is *ad rem,* to the things themselves in their being and because of their being.
This is the ontological force of objectivity. That is
why, for him, the primary role of the copula in the
judgment is not to wed two terms in propositional
bliss, but to bond the mind itself to reality through
a judgment whose content and shape is determined by the things that are. This is to grasp things in
an absolutely decisive manner (*per modum actualitatis absolute*),[86] for it resolves them into the crisis of
being (affirmation) or not being (negation). And it
does this, not because the mind needs to frame
affirmative and negative judgments, nor because of
what things seem or appear to be, nor even because
of what they are, but simply because they are.

The primacy which the term "being" names,
however, is not only that of the first encounter
and of the judgment's final resolution.[87] It is also
the ultimate horizon within which our intelligence
ranges. Our intelligence never ranges so far that it
outdistances being, for nothing outdistances being; and all that our intelligence can encounter
has some bearing to being, or it would not bear at
all. The modern development of the conception of
totality into that of system (Leibniz, Kant, Fichte
and Hegel), while it is not without difficulties
because of an excessive stringency, has nonethe-

less disclosed something that is not incompatible
with St. Thomas' understanding of being. For it is
by its very character as primary that being proclaims its *total* hegemony. Being is not only initiation and resolution, but also centre and circum-
ference: ontological omnipresence. It is, to be
sure, important to clarify the term "being" here,
since a Hegelian might expect it to mean the primitive placeholder with which the Hegelian *Logic*
begins, the pure being (*das reine Sein*) that is so
universal and so indeterminate that it is equivalent to pure nothing (*das reine Nichts*).[88] It is clear
that Hegel and St. Thomas differ about the nature of the beginning, and in the way in which
they develop the question of origins from their
understanding of the beginning. Psychologically
speaking, of course, they will both agree that we
first experience concrete, complex, differentiated
things. But the understanding of the ontological
structure of those things will set the cadence of the
mind's account of their significance. Both agree
that in the beginning there is being. But, for St.
Thomas, that being is already what is richest and
most complete in things.[89] He calls it act: we
name things *being* because they are *in act (esse in actu).*[90] What is onto-logically (not experientially)
first for Hegel is what is most primitive; what is
metaphysically first for St. Thomas is already
what is most complete. This principal difference
in the meaning of being counts in the subsequent
career of the two philosophies. Hegel's onto-logic
begins with a task and a promise: to build up the

understanding of the whole reality in terms of a concrete systematic totality. St. Thomas's metaphysics begins with a gift, a certain plenitude. The world of things is received as manifest actuality; and the task of metaphysics is to refer everything the mind encounters: — things themselves, their forms, matter, qualities, relations and movements, — back to the fullness first manifest in and through the judgment that things are.

Further contrast with Hegel's philosophy is enlightening with regard to two points: the universality of being and the character of actuality. St. Thomas finds in the unrestricted verbal infinitive: *to be (esse)* the expression of that which is shared universally by each and all being insofar as it is actual.[91] Hegel, on the other hand, finds in the unrestricted verbal substantive: *Being (Sein)* the universality of pure indeterminacy within which all determinations of being can arise.[92] For Hegel, determinacy means the reduction of indeterminacy through the inner onto-logical development of the categories of the system. For St. Thomas, determinacy is present from the beginning as actuality in things; and yet it is just this determinacy of the actual that is most universal.

It is obvious that the meanings of determinacy and universality differ in the two philosophies, and their contrast will take us another step towards the centre of creation. For there is something of import in St. Thomas' identification of what is most actual and determinate with what is most common and universal. Because of its natur-

al tendency towards abstraction, the human mind
customarily reduces the common to the minimal.
Thus, we think of humanity as embodying the generic and specific features of being human while
ignoring the particular differences that characterize individuals. Now, the generic is conceived as a
minimum because it is the representation of that
which is only potential to receiving the specific
differences, of that which is determined by the
particularities. This build-up from the minimal is
achieved either by the external addition of *differen-
tiae* (in the Porphyrean manner) or by internal
self-determination (as in the Hegelian manner).
Nothing seems more obvious to thought than that
the more universal or general a term is the less
definite it can be. Indeed, St. Thomas himself
finds in the unrestrictedness of the term its apt-
ness to designate, not just this or that kind of being, but everything that in any way is. The unrestrictedness of the term is not, however, due to an
empty and minimal meaning, but, on the contrary, is due to its over-riding fullness and pre-
eminence. In signifying the thing insofar as it is
actual (or related in some way to what is actual),
the term *is* and its cognate *being* expresses what is
maximal in the thing, since if it were not, nothing
else belonging to the thing would be either, neither what is particular about it, nor specific, nor
universal.[93] There is, then, a certain paradox in
this convergence of what is most common with
what is fullest and most radical and most completive in the thing.

The distinctive commonality is coupled with an equally distinctive meaning of actuality. For St. Thomas, "actual" doesn't mean "factual," since the term does not move for him in the semantic field of givenness which we traced out in the early part of this lecture. "To be in act" (*esse in actu*) is not equivalent to "It is the case that. . . ." For although it may include a similar usage, it means much more. In any event, it means differently. What is more, St. Thomas' term "actual" does not have the same meaning as Hegel's term "*wirklich*," even though the latter term is usually (and not incorrectly) rendered by the term "actual." But the inner meaning of Hegel's *Wirklichkeit* is quite the reverse of the meaning of St. Thomas' *actualitas* in one most important aspect. In the "Logic of Essence" (*Wesen*), Hegel traces out the increasing determinacy within the system, determinacy that reaches a certain watershed with the category of *Wirklichkeit*. [94] He exhibits the career of a content or formed structure (*Sache*) which, as its conditions (*Bedingungen*) come to be fulfilled, emerges into reality (*Existenz*), eventually becoming "effectual" (*wirklich* from *wirken*: to effect). Now this effectuality is the conditioned result of a conditioning process, even though it is the result of self-conditioning. On the other hand, no such result is intended by the Latin *actualis*. [95] The Latin *actualitas* comes from *actus*, which in turn comes from *agens* and *agere*; so that, in calling a being *actual*, we name it in virtue of its active principle, its agency. That is why the actual principle of a being is *potior,* since it is more powerful than anything else that belongs to the ontological make-up of the being. In a word, then, the term *actual* designates a principle not a principiate, a source not a result. As to its meaning (and without adverting to the distinction that must be made in the order of real causality between the caused actuality of the creature and the causative actuality of the creator), —*act* means neither *fact* nor *result,* but *principle.*

St. Thomas insists that act is prior to potency, and more potent, too.[96] In so saying, he knowingly puts his foot upon a path already trodden a goodly way by Aristotle. It is important, however, to point out another path that lies at the beginning of our philosophical and poetic tradition; especially, since it is a path that others have trod and which still has travellers on it today. It begins with the radical ambiguity expressed by the Latin term *potior.* What is it to be potent? Now, this alternative to the Aristotelian way combines commonality with a certain kind of indeterminacy, so that determinacy will be derivative and secondary. Along the Aristotelian path, on the other hand, the radical ambiguity in the conception of potency is disentangled by the distinction between potency as the *capacity* to receive actualization or determination and potency as the *capability* to actualize or determine. This distinction between passive potency and active potency is further resolved into the more fundamental distinction between potency (matter in the order of substance-formation, and substrate in the order of accidental modifica-

tion) and act (form in the first order, and accident
in the second). In accordance with this Aristotelian distinction, the origin of any change must be
sought in the actual principle appropriate to the
change: in the order of being, act is prior and
more potent than potency. Along the alternative
way, however, the origin must be sought in the recovery of an original ambivalent unity, so that the
differentiated orders of things can be returned, in
thought at least, to their undifferentiated source.
This source is represented poetically among the
Greeks as a fecund Chaos, the mother of all
things. It seems to reign in the same mythical atmosphere mentioned at the beginning of this lecture. But it passed over into the philosophical
tradition as well, where it became an alternate
form of the principle of plenitude; for this primordial fullness was conceived neither as material nor
formal, neither physical nor spiritual, neither
potential in the Aristotelian sense of passive
potency nor actual.

Heidegger's reflection upon the conceptions of
genesis, moira, logos, aletheia and *physis* at the beginning of our Greek tradition attempts to show that
the religious poets and the earliest philosophers
articulated a fullness out of which a differentiated
order came by a process of original self-distinction.
At first the regions were taken over by mythical
divine presences (as in Hesiod), and later by the
elemental principles of the philosophers (the Pre-
socratics). The emergence of order led both
thought and being towards greater determinacy.

But in a tradition which represents the origin as
an original plenitude, an unlimited source of being, power and good, determinacy forecloses
upon that boundless source; and so the determinate is always derivative. According to Heidegger
under the sponsorship of Plato and Aristotle philosophy tended to rest content with an understanding of beings as determinate beings
(Seienden). In this view, the distinctions drawn by
Aristotle, therefore, cannot be primary ones, because they are built upon the determinate results
of the process of the origination of things. It follows, then, that the Aristotelian claim to the primacy of act over potency rests upon an understanding of being that is itself derivative, merely
entitative, categorial and ontic. The true task of
philosophy is, instead, to "get behind" these determinate beings in order to recover and reawaken
the more original process by which things come to
be. Reflecting upon the primordiality of things,
authentic philosophical thought is meant to recap-
ture the morphology of the mythical process of
origins. The Aristotelian path is one that thought
had to tread, but it is a *cul de sac* from which we
must retrace our steps to the beginning.

St. Thomas lived too early to heed Heidegger's
advice,[97] of course, but he knew of the alternative
path just the same. Moreover, he retraced the
steps taken by Aristotle by writing commentaries
on the Philosopher's most philosophical treatises.
But this simply confirmed for him the primacy of
act over potency, for he agrees with Aristotle that

it is prior to and more potent than potency: *prior et potior*. We are certainly entitled to ask how he knows this. He tells us that just because act is a first principle it cannot be demonstrated. On the other hand, he never suggests that we must have a privileged intuition if we are to become initiates of the Aristotelian way. Nor is act something irrational, as though it had to be posited arbitrarily, felt obscurely or based upon a groundless belief. Indeed, St. Thomas insists that being is by its very nature most intelligible *(maxime intelligibilis);* all the more, then, is act intellegible, for act is the distinctive character of being. Moreover, the primacy of act over potency is not a mere postulate *(positio)* to be accepted without full certitude, but is rather a maxim *(dignitas)* or maximal proposition, firmly and adequately knowable, even if it requires study.[98] Because act is a first principle, and because first incomplex principles *(prima simplicia)* cannot be defined, it does not follow that act cannot be known. For it can be grasped *(videri)* by the relation *(proportio)* two things have to each other; as for example, how the builder relates to what is buildable, or someone awake to someone asleep.[99] From such particular examples, then, we can come to the knowledge of both act and potency indirectly *(proportionaliter)*.

Not only is the primacy of act relevant to creation *ex nihilo,* but so too is the nature of the order that properly obtains between potency and act. Their relation is not in itself one of reciprocity. Act alone is absolute; potency is only relative. Act stands to potency somewhat in the way in which Aristotle's primary subjects of predication stand to their predicates; for predicates are referred to them, but they are not predicated of anything else.[100] So, too, act alone is in its full and proper sense non-referrable, for there is nothing to refer it to.[101] Within a certain order, act stands for that which is most fully determinate in that order; and in the order of being, act stands for that which is absolutely determinate. Capacity or passive potency, on the other hand, can be understood only by reference to another, viz., to the actuality that fulfills it. Precisely as potency, it has no other meaning or reality than such other-directedness.[102] The relation of what is potential in the thing to what is actual is one of real dependence, that is, dependence for the actuality it has or may receive (participation). Act, on the other hand, can be referred to potentiality only by a relation of reason, that is, one of our own making.[103] *We* can put act into a relation of equivalence and reciprocity, since both of them are terms equally at our disposal; but the equivalence and reciprocity do not preside in the *thing*. In the thing there is inequality and non-reciprocity between the actual and the non-actual or potential features of the thing. Act is related to potency in the way in which the knowable is related to the knowledge of it, and God is related to creatures: by relations of reason alone. The very non-reciprocity that we found to hold between giver and receiver does not hold only between creator and creature; it is also reflected in the ontological interior of the creature itself.

The Aristotelian path leads from various kinds of potency to their determining and completive acts. It is form that actuates matter, giving to it the definiteness admired by most Greeks. It is accidental qualification that fulfils the receptive potencies of substances, bringing them to further completion. And so, form and accidental determinants are what is actual in their respective orders. Because of one or two events that had happened, and one or two thoughts that had been thought along the way, St. Thomas continued beyond that formal limit at which Aristotle had found his highest principle of act. And beyond form, in the trans-formal texture of actual existence, St. Thomas found the absolutely determinate principle of existential act: *actus essendi,* the act of being.

A paean to act as *esse* sounds in his works. A modern editor has gathered together some of the more striking characterizations in the compass of two pages in an easily available little book.[104] It goes without saying, of course, that they should be studied in their larger context. Being *(ens)* is that which, as it were, has *esse,* [105] for being is imposed upon something from the very act of existing of the thing;[106] and so, properly, being signifies something existing in act *(aliquid proprie esse in actu).* [107] St. Thomas indicates ways in which a thing can be said to *be* in the weaker senses that refer to, but fall short of, actual existence *(esse in actu):* thus, something can be said to be in the potentiality of the matter, as fire in the kindling; or

again, in the mind, as the formula for combustion
in the mind of the chemist or the arsonist; or in
still another way, in the active power of the agent,
as fire in the match (weaker in the sense that, although the fire *exists* in a more powerful, determinant mode, *it* doesn't exist in itself at all).[108]
When we say that something *is,* "is" means "primarily that which the intellect apprehends as being absolutely actual."[109] *Esse* is the intrinsic and
exclusive source of what is actual in a thing. "That
which has *esse* is made actually existent"[110] thereby. Any form "is understood to exist actually only
in virtue of the fact that it is held to *be.* "[111]

And so, along the path that St. Thomas has
walked he has found that it is not form that is most
actual, but rather that *esse* is the actuality of every
form.[112] Indeed, of itself, form is not actual; it can
be said to be relatively actual, that is, actual only
through its relation to that which is absolutely and
in every respect actual. *Esse* is the actuality of all
acts, the perfection of all perfections;[113] it is more
formal than form, most determinative and completive, innermost and deepest in each thing,[114]
superior and noblest among all the principles that
compose the thing.[115] Being most complete, it is
the principle of plenitude that is reached in the
journey from potency to act. And yet, it is what
first falls into the intellect, and what we encounter
in everything that we encounter. It is the source of
everything that is in the creature, and the source
of the generosity with which the creator creates.

If the act of which St. Thomas speaks is mistaken for fact or result, the conception will not be able to carry the weight he has put upon it. Only as the most decisive and completive principle can *esse,* so to speak, "draw" all else in the being: — form, matter, accidents, — out of nothing and into composite unity with it. Only in this sublimation of other principles into its own order can their own nature be realized and the being itself made actual. Only in this way can there be an *it* in the first place. Not that the intrinsic act of the creature does this out of and from itself *(a se).* Rather, the actuation in the thing at this most absolute level of actuality *(per modum actualitatis absolute)* comes about through the communication of *esse* to the creature by the creator.

The philosopher who speaks of act here cannot fail to learn humility, for his dry language can scarcely hint at the drama with which the creature first begins to be and continues to be. On this level, the creature is bounded at the nadir by nothing, and at the apex by eternity. The nadir haunts the creature with its finitude, for (as Hegel has shown so brilliantly)[116] its completion lies wholly outside of itself in the perfect infinite. It is not simply limited; it is radically dependent for its very being. In a word, it is, indeed, a creature. Nevertheless, this *it* that *is* is not simply negative. For with the finitude, of which as a Christian he was well aware, St. Thomas also recognizes a *per-seity,* the created supposit. For insofar as *it* is and is an *it,* what has been communicated is not simply act, but being, a being.

There is no doubt that the nature of the unity that is created is at issue. As Aristotle before him, so too St. Thomas speaks of the communication of act to *a* being. The creator does not create an indeterminate world, after the manner of Descartes' suggestion regarding the material universe, viz., that God might create only matter and the laws of motion. Nor does the creator create the System, after the manner of a self-determining totality. Rather, the creator creates beings: — this being, that, and yet others. Nor are these individuals mere particulars that serve an empiricist or a systematic function. It was this latter charge that was levelled against Hegel by Kierkegaard who sought to preserve the solvency of the individual, even though he restricted his defence to the individuality of the human subject. The solvency of the ontological individual, including the non-human, is also uppermost in St. Thomas' understanding of creation.

Nevertheless, it seems to me that the conception of the world as totality is not incompatible with this emphasis upon individuals. To be sure, the world is not some thing apart from its creatures: it does not have its own *act* of being. Still, it does have its own *mode* of being. The world is not an individual. Nor is it a mere collection, a network of relations resting upon non-worlded and private individuals. Nor is it the System of which they are mere members. Rather, the world is that which is built into its creatures, and they into it. For they are built-up in and for and with regard to

the world within which they have their being. The
world is a sort of compossibility grounded in the
mutual existence of creatures. The creator's regard for creatures' being-in-the-world is not restricted to ordinary categorial relations, but is
directed fundamentally to a distinctive kind of
transcendental interrelationship. For the mode of
the world is that it have its being in the acts of its
creatures.

These actually existent creatures are individual
beings. Insofar as they retain their existent individuality, they cannot form an ontological unit in
the strict sense. Their own definitive being pre-
vents them from forming more than a set, or a
compound, or an association of some sort. Now,
an individual, as the name suggests, is that which
is actually undivided; and this is what is meant by
an ontological unit in the strict sense: *unum per se,*
Aristotle's "this of a certain kind" (*tóde ti*). The conception is neither obvious nor without controversy. The chief issue is whether or not unity is equivalent to simplicity. Such an alleged equivalence
is not unknown in the history of philosophy.
Thus, atomism is the metaphysical expression of
the equation of unity with simplicity; and in its
Greek form it shows its parentage in Parmenides'
exclusion of all difference and complexity from the
notion of being. Nominalism is a later logical expression of this equation of unity and simplicity;
and Humean impressionism a psychological version of it. Now, this equation, or more precisely,
this identification of unity with simplicity con-

ceives unity as indivisibility. What is one is not only undivided in fact, it is unable to be divided by its very nature, because there is no duality within it that is susceptible to being differentiated. Hegel has made us aware of a tendency in modern thought to frame a conception of the ego isolated from the world and withdrawn into itself away from all otherness and relatedness. Such an ego is derivative, and its abstract simplicity makes it incapable of generating plurality. He criticizes the philosophy of Plotinus also, because no plurality can be gotten out of a unity that is pure simplicity.

Now, if ontological unity were equivalent to ontological simplicity, then indeed, there could be no ontological composites that are ontological units in the strict sense, such as the substances which Aristotle tells us are composed of matter and form, or the individuals which are composed of substance and accidents, or the beings which St. Thomas tells us are composed of essence and *esse*. [117] At most, such composites would be an obscure sort of compound to be replaced as soon as modern chemistry got under way in the early 19th century. Indeed, the understanding of such composites as compounds of elements capable of independent existence in their own right had become widespread two or more centuries earlier and proved fatal to the acceptance of strict ontological composites.

But, if each creature is in truth an ontological unit in the strict sense and yet composite, then we need to understand how there can be strict ontological unity (*perseity*) without simplicity. Or rather, we need to place the simplicity correctly. That is, we need to recognize that, in regard to creatures, simplicity is not characteristic of the ontological unit as a whole; it is characteristic only of one of its principles. For creatures, the simplicity is one of principle, unlike God whose very being is simple. Now that simplicity is characteristic of the very act. Intrinisically and taken in itself, act is simply act. The traditional formula of the schoolmen held that act is not of itself limited; if it is limited, as in creatures, it is limited by another principle, — matter or quantity or form. Because act is by its nature unlimited, it can be actually infinite in God, whom St. Thomas characterizes as Pure Act. Since it has no duality of self and other in it, act is simple. And just because it is simple, it can be the source of the unity of the ontological composite. This is the truth that is exaggerated in the demand that every ontological unit be simple; viz., that without simplicity there could be no unity. It is interesting that Kant, in a quite different context and with a quite contrary purpose, nevertheless insists upon the transcendental unity of apperception as the necessary *a priori* source of unity in all knowledge. The principle of unity is, for him, the principle of synthesis or combination; but taken in itself, the *I think* is self-identical, carrying no otherness within itself. For it is the simple function by which the synthetic unity of the manifold comes to objective unity.[118] And indeed, it is true that unity must be traced back to simplicity. But we must also come to see that not every ontological unit need be simple.

Hegel is right to insist that a simplicity borne in upon itself to the exclusion of all involvement with otherness is a sterile simplicity, incapable of being the source of any duality and composition. But the act of which St. Thomas speaks is by its very nature communicative and diffusive. He tells us that a being is called *being* by virtue of its act; and that to be one means to be actually undivided. *Actually* undivided: in other words, (1) act is that in virtue of which something is called *being,* and (2) that very act is the source of the *actual* indivision that constitutes the ontological unit. To be sure, act is and must be simple; but, since it is not isolated and withdrawn from all involvement with otherness, it takes up all that which is not act *(praeter esse)* into its own power and thereby realizes the potentiality of non-act *(praeter esse, id quod, essentia),* its potentiality to be actualized in the actual composite ontological unit. So that, act in its simplicity is the primary principle of the *perseity* of the ontological unit, of its integrity and undividedness.

We need to understand how it is that the indivision of an ontological unit in the strict sense can arise; and it is here that the Aristotelian path from potency to act provides direction. Both Aristotle and St. Thomas agree that such an indivision can arise only when that which is apt to receive a determination and thereby be realized in the reception is bonded to and by and with that which is capable of providing the determination.[119] Now,

this bonding is just that of a capacity and its fulfillment; it is the actuation of a potentiality. It is the
relation of a potency to its act, then, that brings
being to be as *a* being. The ontological unit in the
strict sense is *absolutely* one, that is, it is not merely
one in this or that respect, but is one without
qualification *(simpliciter)*. It is not simple, but it is
simply one. Now, St. Thomas tells us that a plurality cannot "become one in an absolute sense,"
unless there be a relation — not of actual entities,
independent units — but a relation of principles;
that is, unless there be an ordering in which all
other items of the plurality are related to one principle as the potential to its act.[120] Since the unity
is that of principles, and not of actual beings,
nothing else can intervene between them, — no
"third thing," no other thing, nothing whatsoever.
It is *ens et unum per se.* And that is why being and
unity are convertible, and why there is an ontological preference on the part of each being in
favour of its own unity.

Act is always the act *of* a being, the being of a
stone *(esse lapidis),* for example.[121] And that which
is not act in the thing (essence) simply *is not* without the act; lacking the act, it simply and absolutely is not. Act is that by which *(quo est)* whatever is *(quod est)* is. The possessive genitive, then,
stands for a non-reciprocal relation of potency to
act in the absolute order of being. For that which
the thing is (stone) is appropriated ("owned") by
that *esse* which, being act, appropriates what the
stone is in its capacity but cannot be without that

act *(esse)*. The simplicity of *esse* has loaned to the composite that actual indivision without which it could not be an ontological unit in the strict sense: *ens per se*. And the act is the thing's *own* act in that the act is the source of the thing's capacity coming to actual subsistent being: *ens per se*. [122] It must be recognized, of course, as has already been said, that the act proper to the existent creature does not do this simply by itself. Rather, this interior communication, which reflects the giving and receiving that is inseparable from the generosity of being, itself arises out of a larger communication of act. Now, this larger communciation of act is creative activity proper; and it is to this that we finally turn.

We have been examining the absolute nature of act, because it is the jewel at the centre of the gift of being that is communicated in and through the creator's activity. Act is absolutely *fundamental,* since without it nothing else can be. It is most *radical,* since it is the root without which nothing else in the thing can be. At the same time, it is most *common* or *universal,* since its proper effect is not merely some modification or arrangement of already existing things, nor merely the generation of a certain kind of thing; but, rather, creation has as its distinctive effect the very coming into being of any and everything *qua* being. [123] In the accidental modification of things and in the generation of substances, creaturely causes play their secondary and limited role; but "God is universally productive *(activus universaliter)* of the total being

of things *(totius esse).* "[124] Now, as we have already
seen, the ontological commonality or universality
(as distinct from abstract universality) is inseparable from the fullness of existential act; so that
act, taken absolutely as *esse* — at once, most fundamental and radical, most common and total, and
most complete in its determinative power — is the
primal principle of plenitude.[125]

The metaphysical axioms of causality are suf-
fused and transformed by this most determinative
plenitude of act, so that they bespeak an absolute
energy *(energeia).* There are three principal axioms. First, the axiom of agency or effectivity:
omne agens agit inquantum est actu, every agent acts
insofar as it is in act.[126] Moreover, what the agent
communicates is precisely, act; for an agent is an
agent insofar as it makes something to be actual.
It follows, therefore, that what is received from an
agent must be just this: act. Second, the axiom of
similitude: *omne agens agit sibi simile,* every agent
acts so as to produce what is like itself.[127] This axiom is often called the principle of formal causality, or more correctly, of exemplar causality.
These designations, while correct, are liable to
mislead at the metaphysical level of causality. For
St. Thomas adds: *inquantum est actu.*[128] That is to
say: every agent acts so as to produce what is like
itself insofar as it is an agent and in act. Further-
more, it is through the very act, which the recipient has received and which the agent has communicated, that the recipient becomes like the agent.
So that the very process of approximation

(assimilatio) of recipient to agent is an affair shot
through with act. Third, it is less obvious that the
axiom of finality also is to be regarded in terms of
act: *omne agens agit propter finem,* every agent acts
for the sake of an end.[129] If we are to counteract
the prevalent modern reduction of finality to
human conscious purpose, it is important to
notice that the end may be sought for by the agent
either in a knowing manner or by virtue of the
very nature of the agent. Our present interest in
the axiom, however, is to touch only that point at
which act bears properly upon this teleological
principle. For it does touch upon it; if only in that
it speaks of an agent, and therefore of a being insofar as it is both in act and acting. Now, the end
for the sake of which the agent takes up its activity
determines both whether there is to be action or
not, and that this be done rather than that.
Natural things are fixed upon pre-determined
results, for the most part, and there is little doubt
about the outcome, providing that all of the conditions are in place. In those acts over which man
has control, the human agent is faced with alter-
natives. Most generally stated, there is a double
facet: (1) whether to do or not to do; and (2)
whether to do this rather than that.[130] Both of
these are factors that preside, so to speak, over actuality and inactuality. For to do or not do is determinant of whether there is to be actual activity
and its result or not; and to do this rather than
that is determinant of whether one thing is to be
actual rather than another.

The three axioms of metaphysical causality
have not had an easy time in modern thought.
Their widespread rejection or neglect is linked to
a redirected interest in motion. The revival of
atomism in the late 16th and early 17th centuries
(Gassendi, Hobbes' corpuscularism) contributed
to the reduction of the various sorts of motion distinguished by Aristotle (generation and corruption, alteration, growth and displacement) into a
single kind of motion: the movement of particles,
whose causation was that of combination and se-
gregation. The rise of mechanism at the same
time reinforced this reduction of motion to the displacement of physical bodies (Hobbes, Descartes,
de la Mettrie). The chief opponent to atomism
and mechanism in the latter part of the 17th century was Leibniz, who sought also to recover a
kind of finality, and who did reinstate a version of
the Stoic *vis activa*. But this same Leibniz in his
Monadology and elsewhere undermined the communicative sense of agency entirely, by upgrading
a kind of exemplar causality to the exclusion of all
real relations of causation between the monads.
Windowless, they mirrored the other monads and
the Supreme Monad. In the question of origins,
of course, the communicative sense of causality is
central. It is not strange, however, in an era initi-
ated by a revolution in astronomical theory (the
displacement of heavenly bodies) and attended by
the mathematization of physics (the displacement
of terrestrial bodies), that scientific intelligence
should quite generally withdraw from an investi-

gation of reality in terms of act and potency, or from causality in terms of the communication of the act of being *(influxus entis)*. What is important, nevertheless, is that the reduction of motion was accompanied by a rejection of all causality except that which was both observable and sufficient to account for motion as displacement. It was certainly detrimental to the continuation and cultivation of a philosophy of act; but also for the cultivation of scientific intelligence and culture as well.

The reduction affected the other axioms, too. The metaphysical principle of similitude is embedded in the whole context of causality conceived as the communication of act. Francis Bacon provides a barometer and bellweather of the new intellectual climate and of the withdrawal from the context of metaphysical causality as the communication of act. He strives for a new understanding of nature, but is not yet ready to quite abandon the old. Of the claim that God created the world, he holds that this is a matter of sound religious belief. He concedes, too, that there may well be some faint trace of God's hand in the world, some residue of his creative activity; but he thinks that it is too faint for unaided reason to use it as a sure ladder in mounting a proof for the existence of God. The old maxim that God leaves some sign of himself upon the face of creation is too obscure and doubtful to be a philosopher's aid. David Hume carried the argument even further, of course, holding that any knowledge we might claim of God from nature would be simply an iso-

morphic likeness of nature itself. A similar and
complementary account could be given of the axiom of finality. It, too, fell during the heydey of
mechanism, and was either abandoned entirely
(Spinoza) or reclaimed for human subjectivity
(Kant). It was another line of withdrawl of metaphysical discourse, understood in terms of a philosophy of act, from the study of nature. The fate suffered by the axioms of similitude and finality was
concomitant with that suffered by the axiom of effectivity; for the three make up a single conception
of agency. As a consequence, the understanding of
agency was altered. With the abandonment of the
principle of similitude especially, the residual
understanding of effectivity or production under-
went a radical reduction. It was no longer understood to be the communication of act in the consti-
tuting of a being, and came to be understood,
rather, as the initiation of a displacement by impulse. As a result, causality itself became so reduced that it became strictly unintelligible within the
reduced horizon of discourse, and eventually lost its
explanatory power. The formulation of laws replaced it as a mode of explanation. The empirical
emphasis upon sense perception was made by Aristotle and St. Thomas in order to arrive at the
understanding of reality through the intellectual
discovery of the intelligible natures of things. With
the denial of formal causality, however, there could
be no natures to discover; hence Moliére's travesty.
Empiricism has other motives for its stress upon the
sensible, for it seeks to describe behaviour.

In short, then, the lines between agent and patient, between cause and effect, were initially blurred (F. Bacon), then reduced to impulse (Hobbes), then to regularities (Hume), or at the last either broken entirely (Leibniz) or rescued by Kant who placed them as *a priori* structures in and of the human mind. Much of this has had its positive results, for our theoretical understanding as well as for our practical use. I have not rehearsed these generally known facts in order to sound another belated chorus of doom. On the contrary, at the beginning of our modern age a new possibility of analysis and a new mode of discourse claimed a certain freedom from the metaphysical analysis and the ontological discourse in order to serve other interests and to perform another work. But interests can develop discourse that either rules out or makes all but impossible the horizon needed for the discussion of questions at once deeper and broader than those that have occupied much of our intellectual effort since the early modern times. The sketch, then, will have served its purpose, if it sets in relief still new and untapped possibilities open to a recovery and development of a metaphysical analysis and an ontological discourse that finds in nature as well as in man both interiority and depth.

I have been talking of this new possibility by its old name: analysis in terms of a potency and act that has been carried beyond Aristotle by St. Thomas towards the absolute consideration of act. "Whatever is present in a thing from an agent

must be act."[131] Causality is communication of being as act, the inflowing of being *(influxus entis)* from
the agent and by virtue of the agent. The link that
holds the three axioms together is their expression
of and relation to act. The role of act is decisive,
since it clarifies the nature of the likeness between
agent and recipient: an effect need not resemble
its cause in some definite way; it need only resemble it in some way. Here again, we have the paradox of the coincidence of the commonality of the
likeness and the actuality of the determinacy. In
asking, Whether the perfections of all things are
in God?, St. Thomas traces the line of similitude
(assimilatio) between agent and recipient, cause
and effect, giver and receiver.[132] Any determinacy *(perfectio)* present in an effect, he tells us,
must be found in its productive cause: this is the
axiom of agency. Nevertheless, that co-presence
of agent and recipient need not require the same
isomorphic formality in both, as when an organ-
ism reproduces another of its own kind and likeness. The degree of unlikeness that can be tolerated between agent and recipient may be very
great indeed. Thus, the sun reproduces its "likeness" in the greening of plants. The burgeoning
plant is not at all like the sun in any strict sense of
a figural resemblance; it does not even behave like
the sun. Nevertheless, there is a communication
between them, as every gardener knows. For if we
remove the plant from the sunlight, it whitens and
dies. The greening disappears; for if the cause
fails, the effect fails. If the cause is there, the "like-

ness" is there, but it is not primarily a resemblance. It is a being-present, a presencing of the cause to the effect in the moment of causation and throughout it. We have, then, not an analogy of likeness in any ordinary sense of the term; but we do have a life-line that communicates a presence. It thereby establishes an analogy of community, at whose origins there is the non-reciprocal communication of agent to recipient. Receptivity, not reciprocation by interaction, is the first response of this community. This community of co-presence by which the effect is related to its cause discloses the proper nature of that which is communicated in and through ontological causality: the gift that is in the power of every agent to give is act. Agency communicates act. "It is through act that any thing becomes like unto its cause *(assimilatio ad causam);"* and this act is nothing other than existential act *(ipsum esse,* being itself). [133] This "likening" in regard to being comes about through the participation of the effect in the power that flows from the agent and its agency; for participation is the same relation as causality, looked at from its reception. And so, the communication of act draws together the three axioms of metaphysical causality: the agent acts insofar as he is in act, the agent acts for the sake of communicating act, and the agent produces its resonance insofar as its effect is in act.

The order of priority and posteriority between agent and recipient is mirrored in the interior communication within the ontological composite unit itself. For within it, existential act communicates the power of actualization which it receives through the creator's communication. In this endowment the principle of act within the creature *(quo est)* realizes the potentiality of the creature *(quod est)*. Because of the absolute nature of the communication between creator and creature and also, as a result, within the creature itself, there can be no pre-existing matter or substrate. No potentiality or possibility lies out of the reach of such an absolute cause and principle. Outside that reach is *nihil,* nothing. The creative communication endows act absolutely: to be rather than not. Yet its product is not simply act: it is an ontological composite, *a* being. In endowing act, the creator also endows the conditions for the reception of act, gives whatever is needed for the reception of its own communication. "In giving *esse,* God in the same act *(simul)* produces that which receives it."[134] It is not too paradoxical to say that, before the created world had begun to be, it was not possible for it to be. St. Thomas concedes that we can speak of the possibility of the world prior to its being created, and mean by its possibility that it was not contradictory and impossible. After all, God did not create a contradiction. But the real possibility does not lie with the creature. Before it was created, there was no *it* in any sense; and so, there could be no possibility *for it,* no potentiality *with respect to it.* Relations need terms. *It* is, simply, *ex nihilo:* it did not exist, it does exist. But St. Thomas continues: If, on the other hand, we speak, not of the passive capacity of the creature, but rather of the active potency of the creative agent, then we can indeed say that the creature pre-existed itself in the power of its creative agent.[135] In the creator, a possibility is nothing passive; it is the determination to create by way of some aspect of his riches, for we are born of *his* riches, not of *our* need. By an imperfect analogy, it was not in the capacity of the oils to become glorious under Michelangelo's hands; rather, their glory was resident originally in the power of his artistry. Creation, as it were, is as though, not Michelangelo, but an infinitely greater artist produces all: oils, and design, and the actual shining beauty.

I have tried to make available some thoughts that strike me as signs of the still latent power resident in the conception of creation *ex nihilo*. It is the conception of the great and continuing "metaphysical event." Much depends upon whether it is true or not, since it directs us to take up the universe as the gift of an intelligent and caring creator; it also directs us to take up our own lives responsibly and with the confidence that the interiority and the depth of beings shine with the benison and the risk of an original and final love. I have left many tasks undone, not the least of them is the great question of the existence and nature of the first principle. But such a task should not be taken up lightly. I have tried instead to accomplish two rather more modest tasks as prelude: to clarify the nature of the absoluteness of creation *ex*

nihilo; and to rebuild a sufficiently rich texture of
causality as an aid towards understanding better
the nature of creative activity. These two themes
have come together in the conception of creation
as the absolute gratuity of the gift undertaken by
the creator in endowing the act of being and its
conditions. The non-reciprocity disclosed by the
absolute character of act, as well as of the causality that communicates act, is already indicated in
the gift. For in giving and receiving we find a moment of absolute gratuity that points towards act
in its purity, and a moment of absolute receptivity
that points towards — nothing. So that giving and
receiving, understood as the communication and
reception of act, points towards creation *ex nihilo,*
once the inherent absoluteness of radical presence
and radical absence has been translated into original act *(esse)* and original potency *(praeter esse)* in
the creative communication that founds the ontological composite unit, the creature.

The several aspects of causality are transformed
by the privative *ex nihilo.* It is the badge of the absolute character of creative power in its fullest. In
the utter contrast provided by this absolute privation, the aspects of causality, — act, form and
finality, — are themselves disclosed as absolute.
The element of power (act) is absolutized, since it
needs no pre-existing matter or energy with which
to do its work. But the original knowing love is
also absolutized, and with it the aspect of finality
(the good). In its freedom, this love is bound by
no conditions that escape it, or that it does not set

for itself. It thereby freely transforms the moment of gratuity in the gift as we know it into its own highest, most intelligent and caring power. For its bounty is uncalled for: this is our absolute privation, and the challenge to receive ourselves well. And its effect is the very being of creatures in the world: this is our *esse in actu*. Reflection upon creation leads us to the centre of the world.

We might wish that our philosophical notions were less encumbered by the situation of our being and the experiences of our life. But the conception of creation draws upon deep and sometimes obscure sources. Now, it is characteristic of important and fundamental notions that they arise in the drama of human existence. This is not surprising, however, for they underly issues of great import that test our intelligence and our character: to be or not to be; to be good or evil; to be free or enslaved; to live or die; to know or not know. These conceptions are tempered by sorrow over evil, by grief over the seeming finality of death, but are also lifted by an insistent hope, or a grateful joy. It is characteristic of such important conceptions that they retain their original tensions, even after extensive analysis. They are, in Marcel's sense of the word, ineluctably mysterious.[136] Not that we are simply ignorant regarding the conception of creation, for we know a good deal. Yet it continues to draw the mind towards it by the power of a presence that remains hidden even while it reveals something of itself. Now this presence is the nature of truth insofar as it eman-

ates from a mystery. For the question of origins is
not to be settled once and for all by verification or
demonstration; but it pronounces itself by its
power to hold the mind and not to let it go. Again
and again, it draws us by a presence within it that
is too deep for such dispatch. In creation *ex nihilo*
the very unity of each creature and of the world itself is given. In that giving, an absolute inequality
between giver and receiver is itself transcended by
the generosity of the communication which intends the freedom and the integrity of the creature. No straightforward reciprocity is possible;
only the receptivity on the part of the creature.
This receptivity is the continuing opportunity in
which the creature finds the integrity already
given to it to be realized in its career, and by the
human creature in his biography and history. The
generosity of the creative giver grounds the absolute character of the act that is given. The glory of
the giver shines as an epiphany in the similitude
between the Act that gives and the act that is
received. The finality of the donation is at once
the good of the creature and the goodness of the
donor. The question of origins has suggested a
path of reflection that carries along towards
understanding origination to be the endowment
of a being out of nothing in and through the con-
tinual knowing and loving communication of absolute act. It is not without risk and not without
promise.

NOTES

* From his general preface to *On the Eternity of the World: St. Thomas, Siger of Brabant, St. Bonaventure,* edd. C. Vollert, L. Kendzierski, P. Byrne (Milwaukee: Marquette, 1964), p. ix.

1. Mircea Eliade, *Cosmos and History: the Myth of the Eternal Return,* trans. by W. R. Trask (New York: Harper and Row, 1959).

2. Charles Lyell, *The Principles of Geology: being an attempt to explain the former changes of the earth's surface by reference to causes now in operation.*

3. Most of the examples which follow immediately are to be found in a useful collection by M. Eliade, *From Primitives to Zen. A Thematic Handbook on the History of Religions,* (New York: Harper and Row, 1967), c.2: "Myths of Creation and of Origin," pp. 83-151.

4. M. Eliade, *Patterns in Comparative Religion,* trans. R. Sheed (New York: Sheed and Ward, 1958).

5. Eliade, *From Primitives to Zen:* for *Enuma elish,* pp. 97-109; *Rig Veda* X, 129, pp. 109-111; *Theogony* 116-120, pp. 114-116.

6. "Der Spruch des Anaximander" from *Holzwege* is translated as "The Anaximander Fragment" in an English collection: Martin Heidegger, *Early Greek Thinking* (New York: Harper and Row, 1975), pp. 13-58, especially p. 15. The entire collection is useful for appreciating Heidegger's interpretation of the early Greek philosophers and his own views on the question of origins.

7. Eliade, *From Primitives to Zen:* for *Nihongi,* pp. 94-96; *Upanishad* III, 19, 1-2; *Ta'aro* (Polynesian), pp. 87-88; Maidu, pp. 88-90; Yokuts, pp. 90-91; *Apophis* (Egyptian), pp. 96-97; Boshongo (Bantu), pp. 91-92.

8. Eliade, *From Primitives to Zen:* for Winnebago, pp. 83-84; Uitoto, p. 85; Hindu, pp. 111-113; Zoroastrian, pp. 117-118; Mayan, pp. 92-94; Zoroastrian, pp. 117-118.

9. The discussion at the beginning of *Laws* X on the origin of the cosmos and the coming to be of the gods, and also on the priority of art and intelligence over nature and chance. See especially *Laws* X (892b). Cf. *Timaeus.*

10. *Isaiah* 29:16; 45:9-10; 64:7-8; *Jeremiah* 18:1-14; cf. 1:4-10; *Romans* 9:19-21.

11. The three have affinity respectively with mechanical theories of origin (mechanism), organic theories (vitalism), and technical theories (artistic or technological modes).

12. *Quaestiones disputatae de productione rerum et de providentia* (Florence: Quaracchi, 1956), Quaestio IV, Respondeo; pp. 93-94. Zachary Hayes, *The General Doctrine of Creation in the Thirteenth Century with special emphasis on Matthew of Aquasparta* (Munich: F. Schöningh, 1964), p. 52-53 also cites Averroes, *In Aristot. Metaph.* XII (XI), t.18 (VIII, F. 143 b-c). For a discussion of the historical question of the relations between St. Thomas and his Greek and Arabian predecessors regarding creation, see an earlier lecture in this series (1939) by A.C. Pegis, *St. Thomas and The Greeks* (Milwaukee: Marquette, 1951).

13. Translated in *The Church Teaches,* ed. Jesuit Fathers of St. Mary's College, Kansas (St. Louis: Herder, 1955), pp. 152-153, from Denzinger's *Enchiridion symbolorum* (24th edn.), nn. 1783 and 1805, which reads in part: "mundum resque omnes, quae in eo continentur. . .secundum totam suam substantiam a Deo ex nihilo esse productas."

14. See, for example, J. L. McKenzie, *The Two-Edged Sword* (Milwaukee: Bruce, 1957), c. 5., especially pp. 82-84; E. A. Speiser, *Genesis: The Anchor Bible* (New York: Doubleday, 1964), p. 13.

15. *Genesis: Anchor,* p. 3.

16. *Genesis: Jerusalem,* p. 15. Unless otherwise indicated translations from both Testaments are from this translation, *The Jerusalem Bible* (New York: Doubleday, 1966).

17. See, among others, J. L. McKenzie, "Aspects of Old Testament Thought," in *The Jerome Biblical Commentary,* ed. R. E. Brown *et al* (New Jersey: Prentice Hall, 1968), n. 77, para. 54, p. 745b. Cf. Greek *ktizo,* Latin *creo,* causative of *cresco,* and Sanskrit *kshi*: to establish.

18. See *Acts* 4:24; I *Cor.* 8:6; *Rom.* 11:36; *Eph.* 4:5,6; *Heb.* 2:3; *Jn.* 8:58, 17:5,24.

19. Thus, *Gen.* 2:7; *Is.* 29:16, 44:21ff., 37:16; *Ps.* 148:5-6; *Ps.* 104; *Heb.* 11:3.

20. Cited from *Protreptikos* (4.63.3) by Jaroslav Pelikan, *The Christian Tradition. A History of the Development of Doctrine:* vol. I, *The Emergence of the Catholic Tradition (100-600)* (Chicago, 1971), p. 36. Or see *Patrologia Graeca,* vol. 8, col. 164; *Exhortation to the Greeks* (London: Heinemann, Loeb Classical Library, 1919), p. 142.

21. *In Hexaemeron,* Homily 1, n. 6 (*Patrologia Graeca,* vol. 29, col. 16); St. Basil, *Exegetic Homilies,* Homily 1, no. 6 (Washington: Catholic University of America, *The Fathers of the Church*), p. 11: "Or, perhaps, the words, 'In the beginning he created', were used because of the instantaneous and timeless act of creation, since the beginning is something immeasurable and indivisible. . . .In order, therefore, that we may be taught that the world came into existence instantaneously at the will of God, it is said: 'In the beginning he created'." Cf. Homily 2, p. 24.

22. *In Controversy with the Arians* (Oxford: 1844), Discourse II, c. 17, n. 1, p. 315f (*Patrologia Graeca,* vol. 26, col. 197): "For God is not wearied by commanding. . .but he willed only; and all things subsisted."

23. *Against Noetus,* c. 10 (*Patrologia Graeca,* vol. 10, col. 818): "The divine will in moving all things is itself without motion." Cf. *Contra Beronem et Heliconem,* Sermon II (*Patrologia Graeca,* vol. 10, col. 832).

24. *On the Orthodox Faith,* Book II, c. 29 (*Patrologia Graeca,* vol. 94, col. 964): "He wills all things to come to be and they are made." Cf. Book I, c. 3 (*PG* 94, col. 796) on the immutability of the creator and the mutability of creatures.

25. *Summa theologiae* I, q. 45, a. 3c; the translation is from *Basic Writings of Saint Thomas Aquinas.* ed. A. C. Pegis (New York: Random House, 1945), 2 vols., vol. I, p. 437.

26. *Op. cit.* (see note 12), p. 59f.

27. *Rom.* 1:20; *Oxford Annotated Bible with Apocrypha, Revised Standard Version* (Oxford, 1965).

28. *Ibid.* 11:33-35.

29. *Divine Institutes,* Book II, c. 9 (*Patrologia Latina,* vol. 6, col. 305-306).

30. Cf. Arthur Lovejoy, *The Great Chain of Being, a study of the History of an Idea* (Cambridge, Mass.: Harvard, The William James Lectures, 1936).

31. *De Genesi ad litteram,* Book I, c. 7, n. 13 (*Patrologia Latina,* vol. 34, col. 251).

32. See the magisterial work of Hans Urs von Balthasar, *Herrlichkeit, eine theologische Ästhetik* (Einsiedeln: Johannes, 1961).

33. *Summa theologiae* I, q. 44, a. 4, ad 1m (*ed. cit.*).

34. H. Pinard, *Dictionnaire de théologie catholique* (Paris, 1908), vol. 3, *Création,* col. 2034-2201; the specific reference here is to col. 2085. The entire article is still well worth reading, not only for its detailed historical and systematic treatment of the topic, but also as providing a point from which to compare the intellectual milieu at the turn of the century with the issues and manner of considering creation today.

35. See *The Gospel according to John: The Anchor Bible,* trans. R. E. Brown (New York: Doubleday, 1966), 2 vols., vol. I, Appendix II: "The Word," pp. 518-524. In regard to the Old Testament background see the discussion of *dhabar* by Thorleif Boman, *Hebrew Thought Compared with Greek* (New York: Norton, 1960), *passim.*

36. *Confessions,* Book 12, c. 22 (*Patrologia Latina,* vol. 32, col. 838); translation by J. G. Pilkington in *Basic Writings of Saint Augustine,* ed. W. J. Oates (New York: Random House, 1948), 2 vols., vol. I, pp. 218-219.

37. E. F. Osborn, *The Philosophy of Clement of Alexandria* (Cambridge, 1957), p. 33. Cf. Pelikan, *op. cit.,* p. 36, who finds it also in Tertullian, who in turn is dependent "to some extent" upon Theophilus.

38. *De praescriptionibus adversus Haereticos,* c. 13 (*Patrologia Latina,* vol. 2, col. 31); *Against Hermogenes,* 21:2-3 (*Corpus Christianorum: Series Latina* (Belgium, 1954), vol. I, p. 415.

39. *History of Christian Philosophy in the Middle Ages* (New York: Random House, 1954), p. 20.

40. Cited by Pinard, *art. cit.,* col. 2059.

41. *Oratio adversus Graecos,* n. 5 (*Patrologia Graeca,* vol. 6, col. 817).

42. *Ad Autolycum,* Book II, c. 4 (*Patrologia Graeca,* vol. 6, col. 1052-1053): *isotheos.* Cf. c. 13, col. 1072.

43. *Exegetic Homilies (ed. cit.),* Homily 2, p. 23: "If matter itself is uncreated, it is in the first place of equal rank with God, worthy of the same honors. What could be more impious than this."

44. *Confessions,* Book 12, c. 7 (*ed. cit.*), p. 207: "For Thou didst create heaven and earth, not out of Thyself, for then they would be equal to Thine Only-begotten, and thereby even to Thee."

45. *Opus imperfectum contra Julianum,* Book 5, c. 42 (*Opera Omnia,* Paris, 1890, vol. 37, pp. 379-380): ". . .quia non de se ipso, hoc

est, de sua natura atque substantia genuit, sed de nihilo, hoc est, de nulla re fecit haec Deus. Non quia nihil habet aliquam vim; si enim haberet, non nihil, sed aliquid esset."

46. Pinard, art. cit., col. 2036.

47. Cited by Hayes, *op. cit.*, p. 58 from *In II Sent.*, d. 1, a. 1, q. 2, contra 6.

48. *Monologion*, c. 8 (*S. Anselmi Opera Omnia*, ed. F. S. Schmitt (Stuttgart: Frommann, 1968), 2 vols., vol. I, p. 22-24). The translation is from *Anselm of Canterbury*, vol. I: *Monologion, Proslogion, Debate with Gaunilo, and a Meditation on Human Redemption*, ed. J. Hopkins and H. W. Richardson (Toronto: Edwin Mellen, 1975²), pp. 15-17 (slightly emended).

49. Aristotle, *Physics* I, c. 8 (191b9-18); *Aristotle's Physics*, trans. by R. Hope (Lincoln: University of Nebraska, 1961): "Clearly, then, [to deny] that anything 'comes from what is-not' means, properly, [to deny] that anything 'comes from what is-not *in so far as it is-not.'* Because they failed to make this distinction, the early philosophers left their problem without a solution; and because of this perplexity they even went so far as to deny the becoming and the being of anything else [that is, other than being itself], and thus to abolish all becoming. We for our own part agree with them that nothing comes from what 'is-not' *absolutely,* but insist that a thing does come from what 'is-not' *in an incidental sense:* it comes from its 'privation,' and this is, by itself, what 'is-not'; hence, from something that does not remain in any product of change. But the early men found this 'mysterious' and therefore held it impossible for anything to come from what is-not."

50. *Monologion*, c. 8 (*Opera* I, pp. 23-24); *Anselm*, vol. I, p. 17.

51. See *Physics* I, especially cc. 6-9 (189allff.). *Aristotle's Physics* (*Physics* I, 9 (192a3-5), p. 21: "We ourselves distinguish a 'material' and a 'privative' aspect: the material factor *incidentally* is-not [what it becomes], whereas what we call the 'privation' is *essentially* what is-not-[yet]; also, a material is in some sense almost even if not quite a primary being, whereas a 'privation' is not a primary being in any way at all."

52. *De Generatione et Corruptione* I, c. 3 (317b5-33).

53. *Monologion*, c. 9 (*Opera* I, p. 24); *Anselm*, p. 18: "[A]lthough it is clear that before they were made, those things which have been made were nothing — with respect to the fact that they were not then what they are now and that there was not anything from

which they were made—nevertheless they were not nothing with respect to their Maker's thought [*rationem*], through which and according to which they were made." Cf. c. 34 (*Opera* I, pp. 53-54); *Anselm*, pp. 50-51.

54. See the usage recorded in *The Oxford English Dictionary* (Oxford, 1971) under these entries: Given 3 (cf. 1); Givenness; Grant 7; Datum; Fact 1, 3, 4, 6; Factum 1, 2, 3.

55. See, for example, Charles Taylor, "Interpretation and the Sciences of Man," *Review of Metaphysics* 35, no. 1 (September, 1971), pp. 3-51. I have attempted to show the anthropocentric preoccupation of this shift in discourse in "Transcendental and Empirical Pressures in Human Subjectivity," *Thought: Hegel Commemorative Issue,* vol. 56, no. 222, Sept. 1981, pp. 272-286.

56. *Oxford English Dictionary,* Fact 4. Cf. the passive form: *fio, factus, fieri:* to come to be (event).

57. See Karl Marx's *Theses on Feuerbach,* especially nos. 6, 7 and 8.

58. *Phenomenology* of Spirit, "B. Self-Consciousness, IV. The Truth of Self-Certainty," trans. by A. V. Miller (Oxford: Clarendon, 1977), pp. 104ff.

59. See his formal treatment of reflection as self-positing in the first chapter of the "Logic of Essence" in *The Science of Logic,* trans. by A. V. Miller (New York: Humanities, 1969), pp. 393-408; and the prefatory discussion in the *Phenomenology (ed. cit.),* pp. 1-57, as well as in the concluding chapter on absolute knowing, pp. 479-493.

60. See the fundamental work of Marcel Mauss: "Essai sur le don, forme archaique de l'échange," *Année sociologique,* N.S. 1, 1925; and (with H. Hubert), "Essai sur la nature et la fonction du sacrifice," *L'Année sociologique* II, 1898 (also in *Mélanges d'histoire des religions,* Paris, 1909). Gerardus van der Leeuw provides an interpretation illuminating for this present analysis in *Religion in Essence and Manifestation (Phänomenologie der Religion,* Tübingen, 1933), (New York: Harper and Row, 1963), 2 vols., generally cc. 50-52 on sacrifice and sacrament, and especially, vol. II, pp. 350-360.

61. "Testimony and Existentialism," *The Philosophy of Existence* (New York: Philosophical Library, 1949), p. 73. Also "The Ego and its relation to others," *Homo Viator: Introduction to a Metaphysic of Hope* (Chicago: Regnery, 1951), p. 19.

62. "On the Ontological Mystery," *The Philosophy of Existence,* pp. 25-26.

63. Gabriel Marcel, *The Mystery of Being,* vol. II: *Faith and Reality,* (Chicago: Regnery, The Gifford Lectures, 1951), p. 31f.: "We realize at once with what care the affirmation 'I am' must be approached:. . .it should not be put forward in any defiant or presumptuous tone; rather should it be whispered humbly, with fear and wonder. I say *with humility* because, after all,. . . this being is something that can only be granted to us as a gift; it is a crude illusion to believe that it is something which I can give to myself: *with fear,* because I cannot even be certain that I may not make myself unworthy of the gift, so unworthy that I should be condemned to losing it, did not grace come to my assistance: and finally *with wonder,* because this gift brings as its companion the light, because this gift is *light*."

64. Cf. G. van der Leeuw, *op. cit.,* II, 351.

65. *Ibid.,* p. 354, where he refers to "Die Do-ut-des-Formel in der Opfertheorie," *Archiv für Religionswissenschaft* 20, 1920-1921, pp. 241ff, especially p. 244f.

66. Marcel remarks, in "Existence and Human Freedom," *On The Ontological Mystery,* p. 60: "Anybody less capable than Sartre of understanding the significance of receiving or the nature of gift cannot be conceived; it is sufficient to recall his astonishingly distorted analysis of generosity: 'To give is to appropriate by means of destroying and to use this act of destruction as a means of enslaving others'." Recall the contrast between the absurdity of existence disclosed in the black root and the clear melody that is rendered opaque by existence (*Nausea,* Norfolk: New Directions, 1959).

67. St. Thomas, *Summa theologiae* I, q. 73, a. 3, obj. 2. Dionysius (pseudo-) Areopagite, *De divinis nominibus* IV, 20 (*Patrologia Graeca,* vol. 3, col. 720); cf. IV, 4 (col. 697) and IV, 1 (col. 693).

68. Ralph Waldo Emerson, Essay V in *Essays: First and Second Series* (London: Dent, 1906), p. 291. Cited by Mauss, van der Leeuw and others.

69. Cf. Marcel, "The Ego and its relation to others," in *Homo Viator,* p. 13.

70. See, for example, *Les mains sales* (Act 1).

71. *Thus Spoke Zarathustra,* Part II, "Upon the Blessed Isles": "God is a conjecture; but I desire that your conjectures should not reach beyond your creative will. Could you *create* a god? Then do not speak to me of any gods. But you could well create the

overman. . . .But let me reveal my heart to you entirely, my friends: *if* there were gods, how could I endure not to be a god! *Hence* there are no gods. Though I drew this conclusion, now it draws me." (*The Portable Nietzsche,* trans. by W. Kaufmann (New York: Viking, 1958), pp. 197-198.)

72. B. Welte, *Nietzsches Atheismus und das Christentum* (Darmstadt: H. Gentner, 1958), p. 24.

73. *Summa theologiae* I, q. 2, a. 3, obj. 1 and 2. On the question of evil, see two earlier lectures in this series: J. Maritain, *St. Thomas and the Problem of Evil* (1942), and E. Harris, *The Problem of Evil* (1977); also E. G. Salmon, *The Good in Existential Metaphysics* (1952).

74. See H. de Lubac, *The Drama of Atheist Humanism* (Cleveland: World, 1950).

75. *L'homme contre le humain,* c. 3 (*Man Against Mass Society* [Chicago: Gateway, 1969], pp. 37-75.)

76. *Phenomenology* (*ed. cit.*), pp. 126-138.

77. See John Wright, *The Order of the Universe in St. Thomas.*

78. Anna-Teresa Tymieniecka, *Why Is There Something Rather Than Nothing?* (Assen: Van Gorchum, 1966), using a phenomenological approach and appealing to "sufficient reason," searches out the emergence of the "real individual" in the context of the world order.

79. *De veritate,* q. 1, a. 1c (*Truth,* trans. by R. Mulligan [Chicago: Regnery, 1952], p. 6). The reference to Aristotle is to *De anima* III, c. 8 (431b21).

80. *Phenomenology* (*ed. cit.*), pp. 19 and 21: "But Spirit becomes object because it is just this movement of becoming an *other to itself,* i.e. becoming an *object to itself,* and of suspending this otherness. And experience is the name we give to just this movement, in which the immediate, the unexperienced, i.e. the abstract. . .becomes alienated from itself and then returns to itself from this alienation, and is only then revealed for the first time in its actuality and truth."

81. I have tried to set forth certain aspects of this sense of objectivity in "Another Look at Objectivity," *Thomas and Bonaventure: A Septicentennary Commemoration,* Proceedings of the American Catholic Philosophical Association, vol. 48, 1974, pp. 86-98; and in "Enriching the Copula," *The Review of Metaphysics: Commemorative Issue, Thomas Aquinas, 1224-1274,* vol. 27, no.3, Mar. 1974, pp. 492-512.

82. *The Insect World of Jean Henri Fabre* (New York: Dodd and Mead, 1966), p. 3.

83. The preceding several sentences are slightly adapted from a longer discussion of discourse in "Natural Imagery as a Discriminatory Element in Religious Language," *Experience, Reason and God,* ed. E. T. Long (Washington: Catholic University of America, Studies in Philosophy and the History of Philosophy, vol. 8, 1980), p. 168; also pp. 159-164.

84. *Summa theologiae* I, q. 45, a. 3, ad 1m.

85. *De veritate,* q. 21, a. 4, ad 4m.

86. *In I Peri Hermeneias,* lect. 5, n. 73 [22]; *Aristotle, On Interpretation* [De interpretatione]: *Commentary by St. Thomas and Cajetan,* Trans. by J. T. Oesterle (Milwaukee: Marquette, 1962), p. 53.

87. *De veritate,* q. 1, a. 1c (Leonine edition): "Illud autem quod primo intellectus concipit quasi notissimum et in quod conceptiones omnes resolvit est ens."

88. *Science of Logic,* vol. I, Book 1, c. 1 (*ed. cit.*), p. 82. For Hegel's conception of the beginning with respect to philosophy, see his discussion at the beginning of the work, "With What Must The Science Begin?", pp. 67-78.

89. In his Prologue to the *Commentary on the Metaphysics of Aristotle,* St. Thomas tells us that metaphysics is the scientific study of the highest causes and principles there are, both those that are the primary causes and which actually exist separate from matter, and those principles which are commonly present in all that is. The former are the object of the science, the latter its subject. Now, this study considers just those principles which are at once highest and most intelligible (*maxime intelligibilia*) and most common (*principia maxime universalia*), and which are inseparable from being as such (*ipsum solum ens commune*). In a word, metaphysics studies "being and all that which follows upon it, such as the one and the many, potency and act."

90. *Summa theologiae* I, q. 5, a. 1. ad 1m. Cf. *Contra gentiles* II, c. 54 (3).

91. *In I Peri Hermeneias,* lect. 5, n.73 [22].

92. *Science of Logic, (ed. cit.),* p. 82.

93. *Summa theologiae* I-II, q. 2, a. 5 ad 2m.

94. *Science of Logic (ed. cit.),* pp. 474-484, 541ff. More precisely, as a moment in a self-determining process, it is both result and source. Reciprocity is everywhere.

95. The closer German equivalent to *actualis* is *tätig*, active (from *tun*, to do; *Tätigkeit*, activity), but this term tends to be more restricted than the medieval Latin *actus*.

96. *In de Trin. Boet.* V, 4c. (*Thomas von Aquin: In Librum Boethii De Trinitate, Quaestiones Quinta et Sexta*, ed. P. Wyser, Louvain: Nauwelaerts, 1948, pp. 47-48; *The Division and Methods of the Sciences*, ed. A. Maurer, Toronto: Pontifical Institute of Medieval Studies, 1963, pp. 39ff.)

97. In *Early Greek Thinking*, p. 56, Heidegger writes: "Meanwhile an epoch of Being soon comes in which *energeia* is translated as *actualitas*. The Greek is shut away, and to the present day the word appears only in Roman type. [The original text has *energeia* in Greek type.] *Actualitas* becomes *Wirklichkeit. Wirklichkeit* becomes objectivity [*Objektivität*]." This is historically correct, of course. What is at philosophical issue, however, is just what has been gained *or* lost in each of these transitions — or, perhaps, what has been gained *and* lost.

98. *Exposition of Aristotle's Posterior Analytics*, I, lect. 5. I have taken the translation made by V. J. Bourke in *The Pocket Aquinas*, New York: Washington Square, 1960, p. 31.

99. *In IX Meta. Arist.*, lect. 5, nn. 1826-27.

100. *Categories*, c.2 (1b3-6).

101. *De Potentia dei*, q. 7, a. 2, ad 9m. Speaking of *esse* as act, St. Thomas says: "Nor is it to be thought that something else is to be added to that which I call *esse* that is more formal than it, determining it as act determines potency. . . .For nothing is able to be added to *esse* which is extraneous to it, since there is nothing extraneous to it except non-being, which can be neither form nor matter. And so, *esse* is not determined by another as potency to act, but rather as act to potency." (*Quaestiones Disputatae*, vol. I: *De potentia dei* (Turin: Marietti, 1931), p. 224-225.)

102. On relative terms: Aristotle, *Categories*, c. 7 (6a36). St. Thomas, *Contra gentiles* II, c. 12 (2).

103. *Contra gentiles* II, c. 12(3-4). Cf. *De veritate* I, 4c; Aristotle, *Metaphysics* IV, c. 15 (1021a30).

104. *An Introduction to the Metaphysics of St. Thomas Aquinas*, ed. J. F. Anderson (Chicago: Regnery, 1953), pp. 21-23. See also his *The Cause of Being: The Philosophy of Creation in St. Thomas* (St. Louis: Herder, 1952).

105. *In XII Metaphysic.*, I, 2419: "quasi habens esse."

106. *In I Sent.*, d. 8, q. 1, a.1.

107. *Summa theologiae* I, q. 5, a. 1, ad 1m.

108. *De pot. dei*, q. 7, a. 2, ad 9m.

109. *In I Peri Herm.*, lect. 5, n. 73 [22].

110. *De pot. dei, loc. cit.*

111. *Ibid.*

112. *Summa theologiae* I, q. 3, a. 4. *In I Peri Herm.*, *loc. cit.*: "Actualitas, quam principaliter significat hoc verbum EST, est communiter actualitas omnis formae."

113. *De pot. dei, loc. cit.*: "Hoc quod dico *esse* est actualitas omnium actuum, et propter hoc est perfectio omnium perfectionum."

114. *Summa theologiae* I, q. 8, a. 1c: "Esse autem est illud quod est magis intimum cuilibet, et quod profundius omnibus inest, cum sit formale respectu omnium quae in re sunt."

115. *In I Sent.*, d. 17, q. 1, a. 2, ad 3m.

116. *Science of Logic*, (*ed. cit.*), pp. 126-150, that is, from the *limit* to *affirmative infinity*.

117. *See, for example, Contra gentiles* II, cc. 52-54. Much that is contained in the next half dozen paragraphs comes from study of this passage on composition.

118. *Critique of Pure Reason*, 2nd. edition, Part I, Division I, Book I, c.2, nos. 15-18 (B128-140).

119. *Contra gentiles* II, c. 53 (2): "In quocumque enim inveniuntur aliqua duo quorum unum est complementum alterius, proportio unius eorum ad alterum est sicut *proportio* potentiae *ad actum:* nihil enim completur nisi per *proprium* actum." (Italics added.)

120. *Contra gentiles* I, c. 18 (2): "Nam in omni composito oportet esse actum et potentiam. Non enim plura possunt *simpliciter unum* fieri nisi aliquid sit ibi actus, et aliud potentia. Quae enim actu sunt, non uniuntur nisi quasi colligata vel sicut congregata." (Italics added.)

121. *Contra gentiles* II, c. 52 (2).

122. *Contra gentiles* II, c. 53 (3).

123. *Summa theologiae* I, q. 44, a. 2c.

124. *Contra gentiles* II, c. 16 (9) and (14): "This truth refutes the error of the ancient philosophers who asserted that matter has no

cause whatsoever, for they perceived that in the actions of particular agents there is always an antecedent subject underlying
the action; and from this observation they assumed the opinion
common to all, that from nothing, comes nothing. Now, indeed, this is true of particular agents. But the ancient philosophers had not yet attained to the knowledge of the universal
agent which is productive of the total being, and for His action
necessarily presupposes nothing whatever." (*On the Truth of the
Catholic Faith, Book Two: Creation.* trans. by J. F. Anderson
(New York: Doubleday, 1956), p. 53.)

125. *Contra gentiles* II, c. 6 (7): As causal principle, "the more perfect
is the principle of a thing's action, to so many more and more
remote things can it extend its action."

126. *Contra gentiles* II, c. 6 (4); c. 7 (3); c. 8 (2).

127. *Contra gentiles* II, c. 11 (3); c. 53 (5). Cf. Cg II, c. 6 (5-6).

128. *Contra gentiles* II, c. 53 (5).

129. *Contra gentiles* III, c. 2.

130. See the penetrating analysis by Gerard Smith, *Natural Theology:
Metaphysics II* (New York: Macmillan, 1951), pp. 141-143. Also
in *The Philosophy of Being: Metaphysics I* (New York: Macmillan,
1961), pp. 103-148.

131. *Contra gentiles* II, c. 53 (3).

132. *Summa theologiae* I, q. 4, a. 2.

133. *Contra gentiles* II, c. 53 (5).

134. *De potentia dei,* q. 3, a. 1, ad 17m: "Deus simul dans esse, pro-
ducit id quod esse recipit: et sic non oportet quod agat ex ali-
quo praeexistenti."

135. *Ibid.,* ad 2m.

136. "On the Ontological Mystery," *The Philosophy of Existence,
passim;* especially p. 8: "A mystery is a problem which en-
croaches upon its own data, invading them, as it were, and
thereby transcending itself as a simple problem."

The Aquinas Lectures
Published by the Marquette University Press
Milwaukee WI 53201-1881 USA
http://www.marquette.edu/mupress/

The Aquinas Lectures

The Aquinas Lectures

About the Aquinas Lecture Series

The Annual St. Thomas Aquinas Lecture Series began at Marquette University in the spring of 1937. Ideal for classroom use, library additions, or private collections, the Aquinas Lecture Series has received international acceptance by scholars, universities, and libraries. Hardbound in maroon cloth with gold stamped covers. Uniform style. Some reprints with soft covers. Complete set (ISBN 0-87462-150-X) receives a 40% discount. New standing orders receive a 30% discount. Regular reprinting keeps all volumes available. Ordering information:

Marquette University Press
Phone: (800) 247-6553
or order online at: http://www.marquette.edu/mupress/

Editorial Address:
Dr. Andrew Tallon, Director
Marquette University Press
P.O. Box 3141
Milwaukee WI 53201-3141
Tel: (414) 288-1564 FAX: (414) 288-7813
email: andrew.tallon@marquette.edu